NØRTH

How to Live Scandinavian

Brontë Aurell

What is Scandinavia?

Scandinavia is a geographical definition, based on the Scandinavian peninsula, and includes Sweden, Norway and Denmark – even though it's not really on the peninsula – but not Finland, even thought it borders Sweden and Norway. Confused yet?

Most Scandinavians would include Finland when talking about Scandinavia, although Finns don't always include themselves in Scandinavia. Some do, but not all. This sometimes causes awkward situations where nobody wants to ask so we stare at the ground and wonder what else to talk about. Then we remember that as long as Finland loves ice hockey, saunas and Eurovision as much as the rest of us, then we're all friends. Who cares what others call us? But, officially, Finland is Nordic, not Scandinavian.

If you talk about Nordic countries (as a cultural union) and the Nordic Council (a geo-political inter-parliamentary forum for co-operation between the Nordic countries formed in 1952 to promote co-operation between the main Nordic countries), then it is made up of Sweden, Norway, Denmark, Finland, Iceland, the Faroe Islands and Greenland and the Åland Islands. Here, we're all united again – even if we are not near each other geographically.

Whether you call us Scandinavian or Nordic, we're all friends and, in one way or another, we're united. This book is about Scandinavia, though, and focuses on Sweden, Norway and Denmark.

Our geographical Scandinavia is made up of three very large places. Actually, two large places (Sweden and Norway) and a teeny one (Denmark). With a landmass more than three times the size of the whole of the UK, we are as different culturally as we are separated lengthways – especially when you think there are only nineteen million people to fill the space, compared to sixty-five million in the UK. The landscape in the north of Norway bears as much resemblance to the landscape in the southern part of Denmark as Scotland does to Portugal; it's an absolutely huge place.

At the end of it all, we are united by the similarities in our main languages, the rich history of our Viking heritage, Norse mythology, all the times we have fought, traded countries, fought again and made up, and eventually ended up as one of the most forward-thinking, top-of-the-happiness-league-table places on the planet. The harsh environment that we live in also unites us – in the snow, in the darkness, in the amazing light and in green nature. We are so very different and we are so very similar, that the delineation between nations becomes blurry. This book is an attempt to untangle some of the smaller things that separate us and to illustrate the big stuff that makes us so very proud to be Scandinavians.

ISLAND

NORGE

Trondheim

Bergen

Oslo

Gothenberg

DANMARK

København

SVERIGE

Stockholm

SUOMI

Helsinki

N

Style

How Scandinavians see each other

From the outside looking in, other nations see the Scandinavian countries as one big place. They don't see Norway, Sweden and Denmark – only fjords, snow, blonde people and meatballs – with some ABBA thrown into the mix. To the outside world, 'Scandinavia' is the brand by which we define ourselves once we leave our shores and travel out into the big world.

If you ask a Scandinavian person how they see themselves, you will – guaranteed – never get the reply 'Scandinavian'. Nobody in Denmark, Sweden or Norway identifies with a collective nationality. Just because it is a geographical definition doesn't mean it is a national one. People in England may well identify both as British and English, but a Dane will always be a Dane unless the talk is of geography – in which case he can be Scandinavian. Or Nordic, if the talk is about the Nordic union. It will never be any Scandinavian's first choice to identify as Scandinavian and we have a tough time trying to understand why the outside world doesn't understand this.

For centuries we have lived side by side and we have been through a lot together. There have been wars, lots of wars. Times of peace and calm and times when we traded parts of our countries to each other willy-nilly. We have, over time, grown to have a loving relationship and deep understanding with our neighbours. This relationship is based on trust, respect and mutual cultural understanding – despite our massive landmass, our cultures have many similarities (both cultural and linguistically) and, to an outsider, perhaps this is why we are often seen as one big nation. On the other hand, despite being so close, we are also far apart and we view each other very differently to how we are viewed by outsiders.

How others see Scandinavia

Here, the stereotypes often rule: blonde men and women, equality, nature, snow, lakes and fjords, bicycles, brave Vikings. The social welfare states, filled to the brim with cinnamon buns and pretty people. Maybe some nakedness thrown in for good measure. Definitely some ABBA, Swedish House Mafia and likely a bit of Nordic Noir and knitted-jumper fashion.

How we see ourselves (sort of, sometimes)

Danes are seen by themselves as laid-back – no state-run alcohol shops, freedom to drink at seven in the morning. Norway views them as the comfortable people – the Danes have time to do everything, no stress, whereas the Swedes see Denmark as lacking in self-control when it comes to drinking and such things. Sweden is also well aware that Denmark has Little Brother syndrome about being the smallest of the three countries, so makes sure to hand out an appropriate amount of loving teasing so that Denmark stays just a teeny bit miffed.

Both Sweden and Norway have issues understanding Danes because they sound as though they have hot potatoes in their mouths when they speak.

Norway regards Denmark as super-cool; the continental ones of the lot. Tall, stylish and always dressed in black. On the flipside, Norway laughs at the fact that Denmark's highest 'mountain' is 147 metres (482 feet) high. Norway also likes Denmark because it is easy to get along with. Because Norway has little idea what Denmark is saying (both because of the hot potato and likely because he is drunk), Norway just smiles and nods and gets along with Denmark that way. It's all very *hyggeligt*.

Denmark sees itself are the forefather of the Vikings, the old ruler of Scandinavia at the time and the true owner of Skåne (the bottom part of Sweden). Denmark's opinion matters and Sweden and Norway can say whatever they want: Denmark knows it is right and is prepared to shout about it. Denmark also realises it didn't actually invent much stuff (the Great Dane is not Danish, nor is the Danish pastry), so sometimes it's not so nice to be Denmark standing in the shadow of the others with all their mountains, majestic fjords and cool inventions (such as the cheese slicer, Tetra Pak and dynamite).

Norway is the most beautiful of the three – and the one most in touch with nature. Despite Norway and Denmark being linked as one for many, many years, nobody talks about that any more. Denmark merely looks to Norway as the blonder, richer version of themselves (but with more expensive alcohol – and ~~better~~ mountains).

Sweden views Norway slightly differently. There is an element of Norway being a bit lazy since they got all their cash from oil (many young Swedes go to Norway to work in coffee shops because it pays £17 an hour). Plus there is an element of Norwegians being a bit too much nature and not enough, well, clean, cool clothes. They eat too much fish. Sweden also thinks that Norway is the confident, outdoorsy one. Secretly, Norway would like to be a bit more like Sweden, with all its cheap food and endearing accents.

Norwegians are easy to love because they are so jolly – their accent just sings out pure jolliness, even when they are angry (a natural inflection on the ending of all sentences does help).

Sweden is the most tech-savvy, forward-thinking and entrepreneurial of the three. The business-savvy big brother, very organised (in every aspect). Swedes have great self-control when in Sweden, and both Denmark and Norway applaud all the good order and rule-following that goes on. Sweden sets a good example to the others, even to the point of being regarded as a bit snobbish at times by the Norwegians. There is a term used in Norway when they talk about Sweden: *söta bror* – it means 'sweet brother'. Nobody in Sweden seems to be aware of this, and Norway is surprised that neither Sweden nor Denmark have similarly nice terms for them.

Danes accept the self-righteousness of the Swedes because they know that as soon as the Swede steps foot on Danish soil, he'll drink himself silly and will have to be put back on the boat-of-shame to Sweden. There is a common set of dad-jokes in Denmark centred around Swedes:

'I'll sing you a song about all the nice things about Sweden' (and he'll play you an instrumental piece of music).

'Do you know why Jesus wasn't born in Sweden? They couldn't find three wise men and a virgin.' You get the point.

Sweden sees itself as the rule-keeper of things. If you can make a rule for it, then it shall be done. Rules for queuing, rules for tax, rules for shopping, rules, rules, rules. Rules create order and Swedes love order.

But deep down, we're all the same, really...

How to be more Danish

Short of being born and raised within the Danish borders, here is a cheat sheet for the downright stereotypical way to live life like a Dane.

1. Wear black, a lot. From top to bottom. It shows off our (sometimes) blonde hair. Add a really big scarf. A black one.
2. Speak on your in-breath when you say *ja* ('yes'), pronounced 'yeah'.
3. Eat open sandwiches on very dark rye bread. Every day. Sandwiches were meant to be topless. Also, top your open cheese sandwich with strawberry jam.
4. Have lunch at 11 a.m.
5. Be *hygge* superior. Because you *know*. You *really* know.
6. If someone asks you how you are, make sure you tell them. In great detail.
7. Get annoyed when people ask you: 'Are you Dutch?' 'No, Danish. They're not even next to each other. What's wrong with you? Mermaids and Lego versus windmills and clogs?'
8. Have an awkward sense of humour and laugh at Nordic jokes such as 'Do you know how to save a Swede from drowning? No? Good!' HarHarHarHar … See also: making fun of everything Swedish. And Norwegian. And Icelandic. And German.
9. You don't eat Swedish meatballs. Because they are SWEDISH. In Denmark, you eat DANISH meatballs: bigger and better and they are called *frikadeller*.
10. Add remoulade to most food. It's a type of curried piccalilli mayonnaise. It goes with everything from chips to beef to fish. E.V.E.R.Y.T.H.I.N.G.
11. Politeness without please – seeing as we don't have a word for please, avoid using this at all times.
12. '*Nå*' – use this word with its never-ending possible meanings, depending on how you pronounce it:
    - *Nå* (short pronunciation) = surprise
    - *Nå-nå* (two short pronunciations after each other, inflect at end) = is that so?
    - *Nå-nå* (no inflect) = relax, please, calm down
    - *Nåaaaaaaaa* = ohhh, so *that's* how it is …
    - *Nååååh* (smiling) = how cute
    - *Nå ja!* = Oh yes, of course!
    - *Nååh* = I forgot
    - *Nå?!* = you're right

How to be more Swedish

1. More coffee. Even if you think you drink a lot of coffee, double it. Go for strong filter.
2. Breakfast: two slices of crispbread, one or two boiled eggs, a squirt of Kalles Kaviar (creamed cod roe) with your eggs. Drink a large glass of milk. More coffee.
3. Be very stylish. Effortless, usually. If you are a Swedish man, favour slim-leg trousers that really show off your impossibly long Swedish legs. Slicked-back or long hair, pale shirt. Pointy shoes.
4. Announce when you need to pee. It really is a thing. At a board meeting in the city? Stand up and confidently announce: '*Jag måsta kissa*' ('I need to wee'), leave the room and do not look the least bit embarrassed.
5. Every time someone says anything about anything, say: 'In Sweden, we have that. Except ours is better.'
6. Prepare a *real* Swedish dinner: *köttbullar och snabbmakroner* (meatballs and quick-cook pasta). Squirt Felix ketchup all over the plate.
7. Schedule your washing time. It's a Swedish thing, *tvättstugetid*, or 'booked washing-machine time', because if you live in an apartment in Sweden, you have shared laundry rooms. Feel more Swedish by doing this at home – just write a note and stick it to your washing machine.
8. *Fika* at least twice a day. Stop what you are doing and go get a coffee. Sit down. Eat a cinnamon bun. Talk to others who are doing the same.
9. Everything you do from now on has to be evaluated based on the concept of *lagom* (p. 144) – not too much, not too little. Everything in moderation (except coffee).
10. Swedify your apartment or personal space: blank canvas, clean lines and efficient layout. Add IKEA. Then add candles and a lot of lamps.
11. It's Friday night. Stay in and do Cosy Friday, *fredagsmys*. This involves opening a large bag of dill-flavoured crisps and pouring them into a bowl. Make some dips. You must dip every crisp before eating.
12. Queue like a Swede. At bus stops, ensure at least two safety metres between you and the closest stranger to you. Do not make conversation, not even about the weather.
13. Keep fit. Two buns a day isn't going to be guilt-free, so take up any or all of the following: skiing, cross-country skiing, walking, hill walking, Nordic walking, dog walking, walking Nordic dogs…

How to be more Norwegian

1. Go for a hike (*ut på tur*, literally out on tour) every weekend, ideally somewhere hilly.
2. Always take a *matpakke* (packed lunch) wherever you go.
3. Every weekend and holiday, go to a *hytte* (cabin). Any cabin. A garden shed can be used as a replacement. This is called *hyttetur* (cabin tour).
4. Avoid looking directly at your fellow citizens in all urban areas, including pavements, public transport and shops. But remember to say '*Hei hei*' (hello) to everyone when hiking.
5. Every summer, go to Syden (the south) for two weeks' vacation. Southern Scandinavian places do not count – it has to be south of the German border.
6. Eat warm waffles with brown goat's cheese at least once a week. When you get sick of waffles, eat a Grandiosa frozen pizza or a hotdog wrapped in a potato pancake.
7. When having a conversation about anything, make sure to say '*ikke sant*' a lot. Depending on your intonation, *ikke sant* can mean a range of different things, mostly on a spectrum of 'Yes, I agree wholeheartedly' – including, but not limited to:
    * *Ikke sant* = yes, I agree
    * *Ikke sant?* = do you agree?
    * *Ikke Sant!* = YES
    * *Ikke SANT?* = you're kidding
    * *Ikke sant* = yes, yes
    * *Ikke sant?!* = I hear ya
8. Celebrate your flag every day of the year but especially on 17 May, Norway's national day. On this day, purchase seven more flags for your collection.
9. Norwegians are born with skis on their feet. Uncomfortable for the mothers, but useful once they learn to stand up and navigate down snow-covered mountains. If you can't ski, don't move to Norway.
10. Sweden will never be better than Norway at anything. Apart from the price of everything (you shall never speak of this openly). Know that if a Swede beats a Norwegian at skiing it is always because of *smørekrise* (the way the skis are prepped) literally, 'a crisis of lubrication'.
It has *nothing* to do with the athletes themselves.
11. Own at least one *allværsjakke* (all-weather jacket). A plus point if it is brightly coloured.

How to be a Friend of Norway

Norway has a collection of Friends of Norway, known as *Norgesvenner*. Generally, this is a foreign person who loves Norway. To be a Friend of Norway, you must have visited the country several times, have spoken well of Norway and probably also have given an indication that you'd quite like to live there one day, sort of.

The unofficial – but prestigious – title of *Norgesvenn* is often given to foreign politicians, artists, writers, singers and other famous people who may pay visits to Norway or who have a personal connection to the country. Once you have the title, it is hard to shake it – and Norway will forever welcome you and be there for you when others have forgotten. Good examples are Linda Evans from the American TV series *Dynasty*, Bruce Springsteen and Roald Dahl (he was born to Norwegian parents, so was a *Norgesvenn*). Bonnie Tyler, Smokie and Leroy from *Fame* also have a place as Friends of Norway.

There is not actual rule book about how one can become a Friend of Norway, but it does start with a deep love of Norway as a country. All people from abroad who love Norway are sort of *Norgesvenne*r, too – but, of course, are not in the *Norgesvenner* Hall of Fame league.

The IKEA rules

Back in 1943, 17-year-old Swedish entrepreneur Ingvar Kamprad set up IKEA. Since then it has become one of the biggest stores in the world with 123,000 employees in twenty-five countries, generating annual sales of more than €21.5 billion. IKEA is responsible for numerous arguments, divorces and also, apparently, the fact that ten per cent of all Europeans were conceived on an IKEA bed.

The name IKEA comes from Ingvar Kamprad's initials, followed by the first letter of the farm where he grew up – Elmtaryd – and the first letter of his home town, Agunnaryd.

IKEA is famous across the world for its flatpacked furniture. You pop into a store conveniently located on the opposite end of town, usually in a deserted industrial area. You enter, you browse, pick up the parts you need and go home and assemble them yourself.

Initially, IKEA didn't do flatpacked furniture – this was invented by one of its first employees, Gillis Lundgren. The story goes that he was trying to get a table into the boot of his car and had to take the legs off to fit it in and, thus, the flatpacked idea was born in 1953. Gillis is also the man behind the design for the Billy bookcase – yes, you have two in your house already – IKEA's most popular product, with one sold every ten seconds.

Swedes across the world feel superior when it comes to IKEA, because they are the only ones who actually understand the names. They will never refrain from pronouncing 'Fyrkantig' the correct way or getting the accent right when saying 'Flärdfull'. A few years ago, a Danish newspaper researched IKEA product names and claimed that Swedes deliberately named stuff you step on, such as doormats and rugs, after Danish places. A claim IKEA denied, of course, but still made us all buy Öresund toilet seats (Öresund is the bit of water between Denmark and Sweden). Finland gets the rustic tables, Norway gets sleek bedroom suites and Denmark gets … rugs and toilet seats.

IKEA stores are massive places, like small countries. When you enter, you are thrust into a maze of beautifully arranged mini rooms that look just like your perfect house: ordered, neat and with no clutter. There are arrows on the floor that you must follow, the maze designed to make you spot as many 'I might want that' products as possible. You won't pick them up here because you don't have a trolley, but once you have seen a product twice, you are more likely to pick it up when you see it a third time – this is basic shopping psychology.

Instead of actively shopping, you get to write down the special number on a piece of paper using your FREE pencil along with your FREE tape measure. You can write down as many products as you want – it costs nothing at this stage as you dream of furnishing your home like the show apartment in the Landskrona section.

IKEA realised early on that the journey around the store was too long and people were

HISTORIEN OM
IKEA
INGVAR KAMPRAD
BERÄTTAR FÖR BERTIL TOREKUL
OM LEDARSKAPET FRAMTIDEN DET RYSKA ÄVENTYR
PENGARNA KNEPEN OCH DEN GODA KAPITALISME

IKEA
DIE GESCHICHTE
INGVAR KAMPRAD
BERTIL TOREKULL

leaving because they were hungry, so they added the cafeteria. Here, you can eat more meatballs than you ever thought possible and finish off with oddly named cakes. IKEA food turns over more than £2 billion a year in the UK alone.

When you are done imagining your perfect life, you will be teleported down a set of stairs to the Hall of Stuff. This is where you get to stock up on candles. Scandinavians who live abroad often go to IKEA just for candles, because we use a lot of them. In the Hall of Stuff you will also stock up on frames, extra saucepans, cheese slicers. There is a close-up picture of hands harvesting lingonberries and you buy a six-person dinner set for £10 just to 'have a spare'.

Once you have filled your trolley with 'stuff' you reach the hard part: picking the right bits for your furniture – all the numbers you wrote down in Hall 1, but have now forgotten why you wanted, but it is TOO LATE NOW. In this area, you often find vultures circling overhead. This is also where people most often decide to break up and plot leaving their children behind.

Then you queue. Like a Swede, you stand there, in an orderly fashion. You buy three blue IKEA bags (useful for doing laundry) and you realise you have spent £692 on STUFF – and one bookcase. You lose the will to live; it's all too much. How are you going to get it all home? You can't take the bus! It won't fit in the car! Who are you going to live with now that you've dumped your fiancée by the Malm section?

And then you spot it – glowing in the distance, at the end of the longest queue in the world: the neon sign, the beacon of hope: *the 50p hotdog*. In anticipation, you hand over your beaten credit card and scoot with your full trolley towards it …

In Sweden, this hotdog is known as the *tröst korv* – the 'comfort sausage'. It's when a 50p hotdog makes you forget the £692 you can't afford and instantly makes you realise you have had a BARGAIN. You start to feel better. In a few hours, your apartment will be amazing. You will have no more clutter and it will be lit entirely by candles. Now where did you leave your fiancée again?

The hytte

At the centre of all Norwegian people's lives lies the *hytte*. A *hytte* is a cabin and these are little places Norwegians hike to or use as a base to hike from, weekends and holidays. A *hytte* is usually made of wood, is often painted grey or red and is always located in the middle of nowhere (i.e. most of Norway). The nearest shop is usually at least an hour away. *Hytter* are always top places in the Norwegian soul for feeling very *koselig* ('cosy') and *hyggelig*.

Certain things characterise most Norwegian *hytter*: Inside, the walls are wood panelling, the furniture is wood, the floor is wooden and any utensils that can be are made from wood, giving it the feeling of, well, nature. A traditional *hytte* will most likely have old copper pans on the walls, some skis, and maybe some stuffed animals. Whatever you eat at the *hytte*, you can be guaranteed it will be served on mismatched crockery – all the stuff someone's mum didn't feel quite worked at home.

Hytter are usually small places, ranging from pretty up to date to rather basic – this largely depends on where your *hytte* is located. You may be in a very remote area, so chances are you won't have access to certain facilities. Some lack running water (this comes from the nearby fjord, well or stream, even if you have to hack through the ice to

get to it), some only lack hot water. Some have only wood fires and take approximately sixteen hours to warm up when you arrive (then it's like a sauna for the rest of your stay).

The toilet is known as *utedo* and is sometimes located outside. It has no lights and, when you're done, you need to add woodchips to your business to ensure you leave it fresh. Of course, some newer *hytter* have toilets and heating and all things modern. Peeing outdoors is a natural part of *hytte* life and you soon get used to it. At one, with nature…

Because of the location of most cottages in the wild, summer is the least popular time because that is when mosquitoes take over and make life unbearable. Peak *hytte* times are Christmas and Easter (when a stay can be combined with skiing, Norway's favourite sport). Most weekends in ski weather will be spent at the *hytte* – even if the cabin is a six-hour drive from your home.

There is plenty to do at the cabin. If you own it, it is a perfect time to do repairs and make things cosier for future trips. When you are not skiing, you read crime novels, play cards. The Yatzee dice game is very popular, as is Ludo. Your iPad won't have 4G and there is no Wi-Fi or TV so people end up playing games. The only way to break up the fun is to eat something, usually waffles with brown cheese.

Another way to enjoy your *hytte* time is sitting outside in the sun to get your face tan going (every Norwegian knows to wear light blue tops for maximum tan enhancement). Any evidence that you have maximised outdoor time means bonus points.

While at the *hytte*, you must also remember to wear the *hytte* uniform: *stillongs*. This is thermal layers of clothing. Wool underpants, wool leggings, wool socks, wool tops. Flannel shirts. Top it with a real Norwegian jumper. Comfort is key, so leave the fancy clothes at home.

Because of the lack of shops, deciding what food to bring for your *hytte* break is an art form. When shops in the vicinity are going to be closed for several days over Christmas and Easter, Norwegians fill up the car with ingredients for all eventualities. There's enough food to keep you safe should you become snowed in or the car breaks down or if someone declares war on Sweden. Despite having the car loaded with food, it is likely that at least once during your time there you will end up eating stuff from tins and that, at least once, you will have spaghetti with ketchup. You will also eat more waffles than you ever planned. In your entire life.

If you don't have your own cabin and you fancy a hiking holiday in Norway, you can rent cabins or book into some along your route. Most of the cabins can't be pre-booked, though, and nobody is turned away, so it can get all-cosy at times, trying to fit parties in for the night. For this reason, the usual Norwegian rule of not talking to strangers does not apply.

The typical Swedish house

From the tourist brochures, it is clear to see that all Swedes live in little red wooden houses with white windows and gables. Usually dotted on green fields, near lakes and forests, the Swedish home is quaint, quiet and traditional. To be fair, when it comes to housing, the brochures do speak some truth. These iconic red houses, while they are not the average house style, are extremely common and popular across the Swedish countryside. Often used as holiday cottages, sometimes they are all-year-round houses.

The colour of the Swedish house is called 'falu red' and is the most famous colour in Sweden, right after the yellow/blue flag combo. The red comes from the copper mines – the best known of these copper-mining towns is Falun, Dalarna, after which the paint is named. The pigment is fine hematite (the mineral form of iron) that is mixed with starch (rye flour, water and oil). The actual colour of the paint varies depending on how much the oxide is burnt, but the traditional shade used is falu red.

At one point the copper mines of Falun supplied two-thirds of all the copper in Europe and, by the seventeenth century, using a by-product of the mining, people were painting their houses with this red. The paint was cheap and became immensely popular. The story goes that in the nineteenth century the government encouraged people to use different colours, so they started painting their houses in other colours, which is why you often find pockets of red- and pockets of white- or yellow-painted wooden houses in the same area.

After removing your shoes at the entrance to the stereotypical Swedish home, you may find that it is filled with older pieces of statement furniture (inherited) and the rest is IKEA. It is certainly no joke that Swedes love IKEA and there is no shame in having an entire house furnished with IKEA furniture. To the average Swede, IKEA represents exactly what they want: practical, clean, attractive. Just like the average Swedish person, really.

In the Swedish home, among the excess of candle holders, you will also find at least one little wooden horse, known as a Dala horse (*Dalahäst*). This is a carved, hand-painted horse which costs around £50. Every Swedish person owns one of these and, if he doesn't now, then he did at one point but gave it away. Made only in the province of Dalarna they have become a symbol of Sweden itself, with each area having its own distinctive pattern with which they decorate the horses. The most common scheme is red with white, blue, yellow and green patterns. These statuettes provide a great income for shops in Swedish airports, where you can buy all kinds of home accessories featuring either a picture of an elk or a little red horse. The Dala horse originated as a hand-carved toy for children, but gained worldwide fame after the World Trade Fair in New York in 1939 (that year, 20,000 were shipped to the US alone).

The Swedish home is cosy and comfortable and, in contrast to the sharp, stylish Danish city apartment, is usually practical and understatedly stylish. It is the bridge between the basic Norwegian *hytte* and the stylish Copenhagen apartment, and perfectly complements the Swedish psyche. And you can add as many little wooden horses as you fancy.

How to make an apartment instantly 'Copenhagen'

When you first go to Copenhagen and you visit someone's apartment, you usually end up in awe … 'Are they interior designers?' you ask yourself. 'What style!' you exclaim, tearing up your insides as you try to forget about your own bedsit hovel with magnolia coloured walls. Then you visit someone else, and you think 'Oh, this place looks quite like Søren and Sofie's'. Third time around, you know: there is a 'style'.

Ten ways to make your apartment instantly 'Copenhagen'

1. Rip up all carpets and sand your floors. Then paint them white.
2. Paint all your walls white. Yes, all of them, white. If there is a shade of white called 'Scandinavian white' or 'Ringsted white' or 'Vesterbro white', go for that.
3. Paint all your skirting boards and doors white.
4. Remove all curtains and traces of curtains, because you no longer need them. If you can't live without window coverings, add some white, stylish blinds, but make sure that, when they are up, you can't see them.
5. Get one colourful statement chair, ideally by a designer from Denmark. Anything with the word Jacobsen or Wegner is good. Buy a woolly sheepskin from a remote farm in Sweden and add this to said statement chair.
6. Have one normal chair next to your sofa where you add a stack of books or magazines with pictures of bearded men. Leave them there.
7. Put just one green plant in the window.
8. Your sofa must be a tasteful colour or stick to black. It must also be simple – none of this 'all the way to the floor' business. Legs – and nothing underneath. Thou shalt not add too many cushions.
9. Add all or some of the following: one rug (can be colourful), one or two designer posters of designer things (drawings of chairs or statues). One standing lamp (tasteful, sleek). The coffee table must be in front of the sofa and it must have thin legs. Two candle holders (the metal kind, from Illums Bolighus). The bookshelf is allowed to be from IKEA, but must be 'Is it really from IKEA or not?'
10. Hide your TV, or, don't have one.

How to dress like a Scandinavian

There is a bit of a paradox here. On one hand, we Scandinavians are designer-focused, fashionable people, wearing clean lines and sporting sleek hairstyles. On the other hand, we hike around in fjells wearing thick jumpers and high-vis, all-weather jackets – or cycle around Copenhagen, dressed in black, with a couple of kids, on our Christiania bikes. The notion of one Scandinavia fits all, when it comes to fashion, really doesn't.

Both Sweden and Denmark have, in recent years, done very well when it comes to higher-end fashion and groundbreaking trends. For years, Norway was left sadly behind with not much of a look-in (Norwegian Fashion Week was permanently cancelled a few years back), but, recently, Norway has joined in with some great new designers and trends and Scandinavian fashion is now very strong.

Scandinavians are practical people and this is reflected in what we wear. Look at our high-street brands: from world-famous H&M, the clothes we favour are simple, easy and practical. Even the higher-end version of H&M, COS, is practical. We dress for comfort, functionality and for look. Even when you look at top fashion brands, such as House of Dagmar and Day Birger et Mikkelsen, simplicity and quality, above all, are absolutely key.

If you ask a Swede to comment on the way the Danes dress, or vice versa, he will see things that outsiders don't tend to spot and draw on the crude stereotypes that make up our friendly neighbourly banter. Are these things always true? Of course not – but if you spend time in all three places, you will soon see that there are certain trends that are prevalent in each and that shine through, even if we – on the surface – look the same.

How to dress like you're in Stockholm

1. If you're a guy, wear trousers a little bit tighter than they should be. A shirt in a light, pastel shade.
2. Pointy shoes. There may be a casual sweater involved – colour matched to complement said pastel shirt.
3. Sunglasses, always. Have really good hair.
Brands to go for: H&M for basics, Cheap Monday and Nudie for jeans, COS, Acne Studios, House of Dagmar, Filippa K – there are loads to choose from.

How to dress like a fashionable *fjell*-hiking Norwegian

1. Layering and keeping warm are essential. No tight layers.
2. Be highly visible, both physically and mentally (smile at strangers, flashing your stylish new all-weather jacket).

3. Wear practical hiking boots that give you blisters on the first few outings.

Brands to go for: Moods of Norway for style Norrøna and Bergans for practicality, sli stuff from House of Hygge and add a Fjällräven backpack for your thermos, Kvikk Lunsj and orange. Holzweiler for when you are not hiking.

How to look like you just stepped off the plane from Copenhagen

1. Wear black trousers. Black top. And a black jacket.
2. Add an over-sized scarf and a very big handbag. Never be more than five metres from your bicycle.
3. For anyone with long hair, male or female, a messy bun on top of your head; very stylish Viking beard if you are male.

Brands to go for: Bruuns Bazaar, Han Kjøbenhavn, By Malene Birger, Astrid Andersen, SAND. Top it off with Sophie Bille Brahe jewellery. For the outdoor Dane, Norse Projects.

How to wear a Norwegian jumper

When people think of Scandinavian jumpers they are mostly thinking of the Norwegian *lusekofte*, literally meaning 'lice jumper'. Lice (*lus*) refers to the tiny pattern in the knit – 'little lice', if you will. These jumpers are also known as *Setesdalgenser* (Setesdal sweaters), from the Setesdal valley where it originated over a century ago as traditional farmers' formal wear. Other variations refer to the Marius sweaters – probably a more well-known design featuring bands of pattern from midway up the sweater to the neckline, from the 1950s.

Iceland has their own distinct patterns on their jumpers as do those from the Faroe Islands. Any reference to Danes wearing these types of jumpers is purely for fashion – it is simply not cold enough in Denmark to warrant them. Swedes also don't tend to wear them and most attempts should not be taken too seriously.

A few years ago, the concept of Nordic jumpers became high fashion across the world. This was largely due to a character in a Danish TV series called *The Killing* (*Forbrydelsen*), where the main detective only ever wore woolly jumpers of a particular pattern as she went about her business, solving murders in the unusually dimly-lit Copenhagen streets. The character's name was Sarah Lund and many now refer to Nordic jumpers as 'Sarah Lund' jumpers. Her sweater was actually made by the Faroese fashion house Guðrun & Guðrun.

Lambswool is thick. That real, thick, coarse, untreated wool really acts as a barrier to the outside elements. If it keeps sheep warm in -20°C (-4°F), it's going to keep you warm, too. Sheep have the added advantage of a thick layer between their wool and skin – and you do not, so unless you wear a base layer, you will be itching all over. The proper jumpers are all handknitted and it can take around 80–90 hours to complete one. Therefore, understandably, they are not cheap.

Your Norwegian jumper, if made from untreated lambswool, doesn't need washing. It just needs to be dug down into the snow for a while. If you live in a place with a lack of snow like, say, Florida, use your freezer. Move the peas and leave it in there for 24 hours to kill all bacteria.

If you absolutely must wash it, do so by hand in cool water and dry by rolling flat in a towel. Change the towel as often as needed. Never, ever hang the jumper up and never machine wash – and, for the love of Norway, don't even parade it past the tumble dryer.

At the table

11 Curious Scandinavian dishes

It's likely that, when you think of Scandinavian food, the first things to come to mind are open sandwiches, cinnamon buns or maybe some delicious pickled herring. There is, however, a slightly darker side to our rich food history. Some are dishes enjoyed only by some of the older generation. Others are dishes evolved as comfort food over the years. Fermenting, smoking, drying … all of those methods used by our forefathers have given us an extensive food culture – from the north of Norway to the south of Denmark, this developed around what could be found on the land and in the sea.

Not all dishes featured here are from the olden days – some are newer and have endured from the seventies when people ate things like glacé cherries. As with any culinary culture, some foods evolve and others stay the same and we pick up weird additions along the way.

Surströmming (fermented herring)

Ah, fermented herring! It's so smelly that you can't quite comprehend just how smelly until you actually smell it and then you suddenly remember all those things you really wanted to do with your life before it is too late. Baltic herrings, caught just before spawning, are put in tins with just enough salt to stop them from rotting. The fermentation takes around

six months minimum. The tins are under such pressure that, when you open them, the fermentation juice squirts out unless a cloth is held around the opening. Some people open the tins under water. Everyone opens the tins outside, because the smell is so strong. *Surströmming* has been confirmed by Japanese scientists as the most foul-smelling food in the world. Enjoy the fillets on top of Swedish flatbread, with chopped red onion, sour cream and new potatoes. The taste is strong, acidic and actually quite palatable, if you put a clothes peg on your nose during the meal.

Important note: if you ever get your hands on a tin, make sure you keep it in the refrigerator at all times, as it needs to be kept cold or the contents will continue to expand.

Rakfisk (fermented trout)

The Norwegian *rakfisk* is not dissimilar to *surströmming*, although it is made with larger fish, such as trout or sometimes char, which is salted and left to ferment in a bucket. Keep it cold for about three months and wait for the magic to happen. Enjoyed sliced, usually with new potatoes, on a *lefse* (Norwegian flatbread) with sour cream. *Rakfisk* is simply eaten straight after fermentation and is not canned. It's smelly, but not as smelly as *surströmming* and can therefore be enjoyed inside without the fear of losing friends.

Smalahove (smoked sheep's head)

Remember when you had nightmares as a child? Those really bad ones where you were seated at the dinner table and someone served you a pig's head with an orange stuffed in its mouth? This is similar, except it's a sheep's head and the brain has been removed, the head salted, sometimes smoked, and then fried. And you only get half a head, usually. The eyes and ears are the best bits and should be eaten first. Serve with mashed potatoes and accompany with ample shots of aquavit. Sometimes, the brain is also cooked and eaten. It is quite nice. This dish originates from western Norway. It used to be a poor man's dish, but nowadays it's considered a delicacy and often served to tourists.

Flyvende Jacob (Flying Jacob)

Back in the seventies, there was an air steward called Jacob. Published in a food magazine in 1974, this is his recipe. It's likely that Jacob was inspired by his travels in Asia and created this magic Swedish dish.

Mix cooked chicken and bacon with a tin of chopped tomatoes, some cream and some chilli and a teaspoon of curry powder. Pour the mixture into an ovenproof dish, top with sliced banana and salted peanuts. Bake in the oven until the banana is browned and serve with boiled rice. One day, we hope to find this magic place in Asia where bananas and peanuts are served with chicken and bacon. And cream. By the way, it tastes divine.

Smörgåstårta (sandwich cake)

In the fifties, when American housewives were busy drinking Martinis and hosting parties, a peculiar invention made it onto the party table: the sandwich cake. It didn't last long in America, but it caught on in Sweden, where now it has reached *protected status of authentic foods that must not be made fun of.*

It is bread in between layers of filling (most commonly, prawns, mayo, salmon, mayo, egg, mayo, crayfish, more mayo). The whole cake is covered in mayonnaise and decorated. And by decorate, we mean anything that might work. Or not. Sliced cucumbers (you can even make use of your spiraliser here), more salmon, lots of dill and other things that can help make the cake look like an entry in the WI's 1972 convention.

Granted, in recent years updated versions of sandwich cakes have started to appear, but for the most part, the more decoration you can fit on the cake to make it stand out, the better. If in doubt, add some sliced, rolled-up ham. And one piece of tinned white asparagus as a pièce de résistance. Found often at christenings, big birthdays and so on, it is served in slices.

How to make *Smörgåstårta*
Serves 6–8 people

Ingredients

Butter, for spreading
6–8 slices white sandwich bread,
  crusts removed
Approximately 300 g (10 oz) good quality
  skagenröra or prawn and mayonnaise
  sandwich mixture
3 hardboiled eggs
300 ml (½ pint) mayonnaise
250 g (8 oz) smoked salmon, sliced
1½ cucumbers
1 tub of good quality prawns in brine,
  drained
1 bunch dill
1 bunch chives

Skagenröra (seafood salad)
4 tbs mayonnaise
3 tbs crème fraîche
1 shallot, finely chopped
½ bunch dill
½ bunch chives
200 g cooked prawns and/or crayfish
(you can also add crabsticks, in which
case reduce the quantity of prawns)
Salt and pepper

Mix everything together – the
mixture needs to be quite thick so it
doesn't run, so hold back a bit on the
mayo at first.

To assemble

1. Butter the bread on one side. Place two slices of bread on your serving dish. Spread the *skagenröra* on top in a nice, thick layer. Add two slices of bread on top.

2. Chop the hardboiled eggs and mix with a little bit of the mayonnaise, and season. Spread evenly over the layer of bread. If you have any *skagenröra* left, you can add this as a third layer – otherwise, top with two slices of bread.

3. Using a spatula, add a nice layer of mayonnaise all around and on top of the 'cake' so that it is covered and all gaps are filled.

4. Carefully arrange the salmon slices in an even, neat layer on top and halfway down the sides.

5. Slice the whole cucumber into very thin, long slices (a mandoline is best for this, but a cheese slicer or potato peeler are also effective). Wrap the cucumber slices in a layer around the cake so it is covered all the way around.

6. Once you have a neat cake, it is time to decorate the top. Use the remaining ½ cucumber, prawns, dill and chives to decorate and make the 'cake' as festive as possible! Do experiment with other toppings and fillings, only your own imagination sets the limits for a real *smörgåstårta*!

Gammel Dansk

Not so much a dish as a drink, although, for some Danish people, it's a way to get out of bed in the morning! A bitter dram made from a secret blend of twenty-eight herbs, this tipple comes in at 38 per cent alcohol, tastes like tar and will help get the blood flowing on a winter's morning.

If anyone offers you a shot of *Gammel Dansk* at the breakfast table, this is perfectly acceptable in Denmark. Be warned, it's not for the faint-hearted, but at least you will feel the warmth inside.

Blodpalt (blood dumpling)

A dish that originates in the north of Sweden, this is the blood of either pig or reindeer, mixed with rye or barley flour and allowed to sit overnight to soak. Then mashed potato is added and it is formed into large dumplings that are then boiled and served with fried pork. A more common version is simply *palt*, made with grated raw potato mixed with the flour, and formed into dumplings with pork mince in the middle. These are also boiled, then served with lingonberry jam – and always a cold glass of milk on the side. A similar Norwegian dish is *Komle* (or *Raspeball*).

Lutfisk (lye fish)

As the name suggests, this dish is fish in lye. Yes, the stuff you can use to make things go 'boom'. It's strong. Most people buy *lutfisk* ready prepared nowadays as few families have a stash of food-grade lye in their larder. The cod is soaked for four or five days in water, then it is soaked for a few more days in lye/water. The fish swells up because of the chemicals and goes a bit jelly-like. After a further four or five days' soaking in water the fish can be cooked. If you forget about the last bit of soaking, you won't be able to eat it – it is essential to remove the lye. This is usually served at Christmas with bacon. The taste is very mild if it has been soaked and rinsed properly, so as long as your chef is capable, you have little to fear.

Spaghetti with ketchup

Look, we're aware it's not really a dish and if you tell any Italians what we do with their spaghetti, they are likely never to talk to us again. A good dollop of ketchup on top of your spaghetti – that is how Mamma used to feed us. In Sweden, they go one better. They have *snabbmakaroner* – quick-cook macaroni – because they don't have the patience to wait eight minutes so they developed a three-minute pasta. Italy, please forgive us for bastardising your national food. Also, we put ketchup in our lasagne sauce. And in our beef ragù. Sorry again.

Swedish pizza

Dear Italy, we haven't finished yet. So, some decades ago Sweden entered the pizza restaurant game. We didn't know that much about traditional Italian pizza back then, so we welcomed the new style of pizza with open arms. Today, in Sweden, Swedish pizza, as it is now known, has about as much to do with Italian pizza as caramel mochaccino has to do with Italian coffee. But we love it. It's what Swedish people abroad get homesick for.

Toppings such as prawn, peanut and curry are common. Kebab meat. Dressings. Bolognese (or something resembling it). Canned fruit? No problem. All Swedish pizzas are served with something called *pizzasallad.* This is a lightly pickled white cabbage salad with oregano and peppers. It has nothing to do with pizza, but it comes with the pizza, hence the name. It is illegal to eat Swedish pizza without *pizzasallad.*

Fiskeboller (fish balls)

Really, these are fish dumplings, but fish balls makes them sound so much more peculiar. They are cooked, then stuffed into a tin with a sauce, which could be dill, lobster, cream, etc. Quick and easy and rather nutritious, just heat and serve with potato in some form.

Scandinavia's national dishes

From the Arctic Circle to the south of Scandinavia, the cuisines are as diverse and colourful as our countries. So when you think about national dishes, you need to do so bearing in mind just how different the dishes of northern Scotland are to those of Seville. Most non-Scandinavians are happy to name Scandinavia as a union, and label everybody the same: 'Ah, those Scandinavians, they eat herring'. Well, yes, we do, but that is like saying 'Those French, they eat snails'.

Some foods link us together in unity – from way back when King Harald was a nipper. Our love of fish, in particular, pickled fish and smoked fish. Fish that could be preserved and last through the long winter months. Bread that could be stored and last the journey to England on the longship. Our love of all things potato is something we have in common but, to be honest, the landscapes of northern Norway harvest little of the same as southern Denmark. Here is a quick guide:

Denmark

The flat lands, full of pigs. More pigs than people, by the way – and pork does feature in the favourite dishes. In 2014, 60,000 votes were cast to find the national dish of Denmark. Fried thick-sliced bacon with parsley sauce won – a dish most Danes wouldn't dream of serving to friends, let alone share with tourists. Open sandwiches came in at number two. Of the eight finalists, seven were pork based. Meatballs didn't make the top ten.

What to order if you want the national dish: *Stegt flæsk med persillesovs* (fried thick-sliced bacon with new potatoes and parsley sauce); in recent years available in some restaurants in the capital. You can usually get this dish in local places out in the sticks as a lunch option.

What to ask for if you want a true home-cooked wonder: *Flæskesteg med brun sovs og rødkål* (roast pork with serious crackling, brown, thick gravy, red cabbage – plus caramelised potatoes, if served at Christmas).

What to eat as a tourist: *Smørrebrød* (open sandwiches).

Stay away from: Most food is safe, there are few scary dishes.

Sweden

The thing about Sweden is it's all mainly about *sill* (herring) and *potatis* (potatoes). At Christmas, add a bit of pork, for Midsummer, some green salads. But really, *sill och potatis* is eaten all the time, with slight seasonal variations. Go to IKEA, and you will be told the Swedish national dish is meatballs with mash and gravy. Also sort of true. Sometimes, it's even *sill, potatis* and *köttbullar* (meatballs), but combined, it is known as *smörgåsbord*.

If Swedes themselves could choose, there is a possibility they might choose tacos. Sweden is a big place and dishes vary so much by region, it is truly hard to narrow it down. There hasn't been a poll to discover the national dish, but let's go with Swedish meatballs, lingonberries and mash – it's a safe bet.

What to order if you want the national dish: *Köttbullar med mos och lingonsylt* (meatballs with mash and lingonberries).

What to ask for if you want a true home-cooked wonder: *Korv stroganoff* (Falu sausage stew with rice).

What to eat as a tourist: *Räkor* (shell-on prawns), if near the water.

Stay away from: Swedish pizza or fermented fish in a tin.

Norway

Since 1972, Norway's national dish has been *fårikål* – stewed mutton and cabbage. *Får* means mutton, *kål* means cabbage. No longer, said the Norwegians in 2014, and launched a countrywide search for the new national dish. One must change with the times. Except nobody wanted to change and, despite all sorts of exciting suggestions, people decided … mutton and cabbage. Better the Devil you know.

What to order if you want the national dish: *Fårikål.*
What to ask for if you want a true home-cooked wonder: *Pinnekjøtt* (dried rack of lamb) at Christmas, *køttkaker* (Norwegian-style meatballs) and potatoes.
What to eat as a tourist: Anything fish and seafood. If you are going to eat out in Norway, you will pay a lot, whether you have a pizza or a proper meal. Go all out and eat well.
Stay away from: Anything that resembles a sheep's head or has been steeped in lye.

Fika (fee-ka)

Anyone who has Swedish friends will most likely be familiar with the word *fika,* mainly because Swedes tend to use it all the time. This is because when they are struggling to find the right word in another language, they just use *'fika'*.

Simply put, *fika* means to sit down, have a chit-chat, coffee and something baked. You can also have tea or another non-alcoholic drink, but coffee is standard. More than a coffee break, but less than something formal, it is an important part of the culture both in terms of how the day is structured and the kind of people the Swedes are.

During a working day, Swedes will usually have two *fika* breaks: one mid-morning (around 9.30) and one in the afternoon (around 2.30). Even if it is a quick one, you always sit down. It's break time, although in some modern offices, people have started to *fika* at their desks.

Confusingly – and helpfully – *fika* is both a noun and a verb. You can take a *fika* or you can *fika* with someone. It is also something you can do with your best friend, colleague, family – and you can even arrange a *fika* date with that handsome boy you like, which is like a real date but with a lot less commitment as *fika* is always casual. Usually during the day, it does not involve alcohol. You can *fika* in the evenings, but then it's *kvällsfika,* evening *fika*, and usually done at home and involving bread and cheese (but still coffee).

To *fika* effectively, most people will indulge in the Scandinavian way of fitting in as much coffee into their day as is humanly possible without looking like a wired tarsier. Scandinavians drink more coffee than anyone else in the world. Think strong, filtered coffee, served in massive mugs. Pop round for *fika* at someone's house and there will be a pot of coffee on the table. *'Skulle du vilja ha en påtår?'* they'll ask, meaning 'Do you want a top-up?' (you do, because you're polite). It's a wonder Scandinavians get any sleep at all, really, and quite possibly the reason we survive the long, dark winters.

To go with your super-strength cup of diesel, you need something baked. *Fikabröd,* literally *'fika* bread', describes a whole range of possible options – the most infamous of which is the cinnamon bun. These are yeast-based buns, because it's all about the goodness of the solid home baking. If you don't fancy a cinnamon bun, go for a slice of soft bread with butter and cheese – or opt for a slice of cake, a muffin, or a biscuit, if you are not so hungry. Mostly, though, it's a form of a bun, usually involving some cinnamon/cardamom/vanilla.

Weekdays, people *fika* at work or after school. At weekends, they *fika* at each other's houses or in cafés. You can, however, also *fika* outdoors, for example when skiing in the fjells. This usually involves a thermos of coffee, some home-baked buns and then finding a cosy spot in the snow to park the skis.

Filling the coffee table

One of the most popular baking books in Sweden is called *Sju Sorters Kakor* (*Seven Kinds of Biscuit*). It was published in 1945 after a supermarket asked readers to send in their favourite recipes. More than 8,000 suggestions and recipes were submitted and a collection of 300 of the best and most popular Swedish recipes for bakes and cakes were chosen. The book went on to become a bestseller – today, in its eighty-fourth edition, it is still in print and remains Sweden's bestselling baking book.

Every household in Sweden owns several old, sticky-paged copies of this book and, seeing as nobody ever seems to throw the handed-down copies out, this average increases year by year. Sweden is in danger of submerging into the sea one day, under the sheer weight of copies of *Sju Sorters Kakor* still in circulation.

The concept of seven kinds of biscuit stems from further back than the cookbook, however – right back to the late 1800s. There had been a period of prohibition but people were once again permitted to drink coffee. They started to meet and would bring along baked goods to go with the coffee; the households that could provide the best kind of baked goods would be considered superior. Essentially, this was a way for women to show off their baking skills, with ovens in the homes becoming more common.

Initially, simple selections of biscuits were offered but soon coffee parties, known as *kafferep*, were happening all over Sweden. Seven became the minimum number of kinds of biscuit that could be offered without appearing stingy, but offering beyond this number would be considered pompous. The seven referred to biscuits only and didn't include any other cakes or buns also on offer.

Also around the late 1800s, further south in Denmark in the area of Sønderjylland, bordering Germany, the 1864 war meant that Denmark had come under German rule. The Germans had forbidden the Danes from meeting in taverns and consuming alcohol so people had to find ways to meet up to plot against their rulers. The Germans still allowed meeting up for coffee, so the Danes started gathering in Community Houses, bringing home-baked cakes and coffee. The women of the town would bring elaborate cakes to the meetings, each one trying to outdo the next and, as these gatherings grew so too did the tradition of *kaffebord* – coffee table.

During the Second World War, this tradition once more became popular among the Sønderborg Danes as the Germans again forbade public meetings – but not community gatherings with cakes and coffee.

A traditional south Jutland coffee table (*Sønderjysk kaffebord*) must have seven types of biscuits and cookies as well as seven types of soft cakes (layer cakes and pastries). Ranging from the delicious rye bread layer cakes traditionally made in the south of Denmark to the Danish Kringler pastries, larger tray bakes and mountains of biscuits.

There are strict guidelines on how one eats these cakes. First, start with a *bundlag* – a base layer – of soft buns spread with butter. Then take a slice of everything. You don't get to select just a few – no, you must taste it all so as not to offend any of the housewives who have baked for the event.

The southern Jutland coffee table is a wonderful part of Danish food heritage and over the past decade it has re-surfaced and become popular again after a time out of the spotlight. In Sønderjylland, you can find coffee tables at the fancier cafés and hotels as well as at bigger celebrations such as weddings, christenings and significant birthdays.

Kanelbullar

One of the most popular exports of Scandinavian cuisine is the humble cinnamon bun. Sweet, sticky, aromatic and extremely moreish, the soft wheat bun is synonymous with home baking and comfort food. It's entirely understandable why the cinnamon bun – or *kanelbulle*, as it is known in Sweden – is so easy to love. The addictive spices are guaranteed to fill your home with scents of Christmas and memories of the best days of your life at any time of the year. Buns don't have seasons, they are for every week and are great to eat in the morning, mid-morning, mid-afternoon and in the evening. Very few people don't like *kanelbullar*.

In Sweden, 4 October is known as the Day of the Cinnamon Bun. On this day, people eat more buns than usual – and a Swedish tourist website claims that the average Swede consumes 316 buns of various fillings bought from bakeries (so not including any home-baked buns) a year. Buns are not only delicious, but also big business, both for bakeries and fitness centres.

In Denmark, cinnamon rolls sometimes mean Danish pastry cinnamon swirls, in which case they might be called *kanelsnurrer* – cinnamon twists. In Sweden and Norway, if the buns are twisted into a knot, rather than rolled, they may also be referred to as *kanelsnurrer*. Some people add nibbed sugar before baking, others add it afterwards, with a sugar wash. In Scandinavia, cinnamon rolls are *never* covered in sticky icing.

The secret to making excellent cinnamon buns is *love*. That sounds a little silly, perhaps, but it is actually true. This is why no two people's buns taste the same – it comes from which recipe you use, how you mix the dough, whether you knead by hand or use a machine. People tend to start with a basic recipe, adding their own tricks and knacks of rolling or twisting. Over time, the recipe becomes their own and nobody can recreate it just the same way. This is also why Mamma's *bullar* always taste the best.

Kanelbullar (Swedish cinnamon buns)
Makes 30 buns

Ingredients

50 g (2 oz) fresh yeast or 25 g (1 oz)
  active dried yeast
Pinch sugar (if using dried yeast)
500 ml (17 fl oz) whole milk
75 g (3 oz) sugar
3 teaspoons ground cardamom
Approximately 800 g–1 kg (1 lb 10 oz– 2
  lb) strong bread flour, plus extra for
  dusting
1 teaspoon salt
175 g (6 oz) butter, really soft
1 egg plus extra for brushing

Filling
175 g (6 oz) soft butter, softened
1 tablespoon plain flour
3 tablespoons ground cinnamon
1 teaspoon ground cardamom
1 teaspoon vanilla sugar
100 g (3½ oz) caster sugar
100 g (3½ oz) light brown sugar

Topping
Agave nectar or dark syrup, for brushing
Pearl sugar, crushed sugar cubes or
  chopped nuts, for topping

1. To make the filling, cream ingredients together in a small bowl and set aside.

2. If you are using dried yeast, gently heat the milk in a saucepan to 36–37°C (98–100°F), so it is finger warm, but not hot, then pour into a bowl, add a pinch of sugar and the dried yeast and whisk. Cover the bowl with clingfilm and leave in a warm place to activate for about 15 minutes.

3. If you are using fresh yeast, gently heat the milk in a saucepan to 36–37°C (97– 98°F), any hotter and the yeast will die. Add the milk and fresh yeast to a bowl and stir until dissolved.

4. I recommend using a stand mixer with the dough hook attached for this recipe. Start the machine and add the sugar to the milk mixture and allow to dissolve for a minute or two, then add the ground cardamom.

5. Add around 700 g (1 lb 7 oz) of the flour and stir, then add the salt, the softened butter and the egg. Keep the speed on medium and allow the dough to start forming. Add more flour as needed – you may need more or less than stated.

6. Keep kneading for about 5 minutes if using a mixer (longer if doing it by hand). Keep adding flour until you have a smooth mixture. When the dough starts to come away from the side of the bowl as you mix, there is enough flour in it.

7. Leave the dough in a bowl, cover with a tea towel or clingfilm and allow to rise for 30–45 minutes until doubled in size.

8. Turn out the dough onto a lightly floured surface. Using your hands, knead the dough and work in more flour if needed. The dough has enough flour when it starts to let go of the sides of the bowl. Cut the dough into two equal portions.

9. Using a rolling pin, roll out one piece of dough to a 40 x 50 cm (16 x 20 inch) rectangle.

10. Spread half the filling across the dough in an even, thin layer.

11. To make traditional swirls, simply roll the dough lengthways into a long roll and cut into 15 pieces, place on a lined baking tray, and leave – covered – to rise for another 20 minutes. Repeat with the second piece of dough.

12. If you are making cinnamon twists, fold the dough over twice and cut into 15 equal-sized strips. Twist each one around itself and place on a lined baking tray. Always make sure all ends are tucked underneath or they will unravel during baking. Leave to rise for 20 minutes while you repeat the process with the second piece of dough.

13. Preheat the oven to 200°C (400°F, Gas Mark 6). Brush the buns lightly with beaten egg, then bake for 7–9 minutes or until golden and cooked through.

14. Meanwhile, gently heat the agave nectar or syrup in a small saucepan until it is just warm.

15. Remove the buns from the oven and immediately brush lightly with the agave nectar or syrup, then sprinkle over the sugar or nuts and cover the tray with a clean, slightly damp tea towel. This prevents the buns from going dry.

This is a recipe large enough for a class of schoolkids. You can halve it or, better still, make the full batch and freeze half. They freeze well, but do not keep long so either eat on the day of making or freeze.

Salty liquorice

A favourite pastime of Scandinavians is to make people from other countries eat salty liquorice. We find this really amusing, watching them squirm as they feel the hit from the insane salty flavours. 'Oh, didn't you like that one? Let's try this instead, this one is called Jungle Scream … No, it isn't that bad, promise …' Once in while, we convert someone to the dark side, but more often than not people just get really cross. It is hard for us to comprehend why someone would not like salty liquorice when it is obviously one of the best tastes in the world.

The Nordic love affair with liquorice goes back a long way, as it does in many countries to the use of liquorice for medicinal purposes. Liquorice cough medicines traditionally contained ammonium chloride, which gives the salty taste, because this helps release mucus. By the 1930s, the liquorice and salt combo had moved on to being sold as a common confectionery in Finland.

Another theory is that our love affair with salt goes back to our Viking ancestors preserving and curing foods for the long winters, so salt has become part of our preferred tastes over centuries. Liquorice with salt is a natural combination for us and one that a lot of us seem to like.

What most people think is salt isn't actually salt at all – it is salt of Ammon, more commonly known as ammonium chloride. In Latin, this is *sal ammoniacus*, from which the Finnish word *salmiakki* is derived. All over Scandinavia, salty liquorice is called *salmiakki* rather than ammonium chloride – it sounds less like you've raided the contents of your medicine cabinet.

The more into *salmiakki* liquorice you become – and the taste buds for this will continue to develop over time – the more you want it. The usual content of *salmiakki* in Scandinavian confectionery is around six–seven per cent, whereas most other places have one per cent content for salty liquorice. A few years ago, the EU tried to set a limit of 0.3 per cent for use of ammonium chloride in food, but was met with a frosty reception up north and this was not enforced in confectionery or ice cream. We're still free to make strong stuff, for now.

The top ones on the list are the Turkish Pepper, the Jungle Screams and the Salty Piratos. Master these and you're on your way and there's no going back: you have gone Scandi.

Open sandwiches

The Scandinavian words for 'open sandwich' (*smørrebrød* in Danish, *smørbrød* in Norwegian and *smörgås* in Swedish) literally mean 'buttered bread'. Scandinavia is famous for open sandwiches. Cafés, restaurants and even *smørrebrød* takeaway shops offer many different varieties – often elaborately decorated pieces of rye bread, piled high with seriously delicious toppings.

Smørrebrød as it is known today became popular in Denmark in the late 1800s when people started eating out of the home. It was a way for the working man to enjoy a substantial lunch by piling high plentiful and affordable toppings on filling rye bread. Rye bread both on top and as a base would be very hard to digest so it remained 'open'. In the 1890s, it became fancy fare for the upper classes and over the next decades, *smørrebrød* became a staple lunch dish at cafés and restaurants.

There are several varieties of *smørrebrød* – split into party, lunch, handheld and lunchbox.

First, the stuff the tourist bureau wants to sell you. It's super-pretty and you eat it in cafés and restaurants, for lunch – always with a knife and fork. This is the same version you may order for get-togethers like birthday celebrations in the office. Called *højtbelagt*, it means 'highly decorated'. It's the king of open sandwiches. The most famous place in Copenhagen, Ida Davidsen, has a menu of 190 different kinds of open sandwich.

Second, there is the stuff you make at home. A little less fancy, not as much mayo and other fillers, this is more wholesome. This is just called *smørrebrød* and is eaten for lunch.

Lastly, you have the open sandwiches for your *madpakke* (*matpakke*). These are lovely open sandwiches you make at home, then carefully put into your lunchbox using special open-sandwich paper (*matpakkepapir*) that you buy in the supermarket to layer between your sandwiches. It will all squash before you eat it and your liver pâté is likely to be mixed with your cheese, but that never killed anyone. This is the kind that kids will have in their packed lunch at school.

There is a three-year training course in Denmark to be educated in the art of making *smørrebrød* open sandwiches. When you finish this, you are qualified as an 'Open Sandwich Maiden' (*Smørrebrødsjomfru*). Even today, people can choose to specialise as a general chef or an open sandwich chef – usually you don't get to be both.

Most of the classic open sandwiches in Denmark are made on dark rye bread. In Sweden and Norway, where they don't eat bread that dark, a lighter crustier bread is used. For seafood, in all places, lighter bread is used. There are numerous classic combinations, but the main thing to remember is:

1. Bread base
2. Fat or butter
3. Add protein of choice (main ingredient)
4. Add toppings for additional flavour, crunch, texture and, of course, to make it pretty

The real beauty of the open sandwich is that it means you eat less bread overall – and in many cases, better bread, too. Open sandwiches are filling without making you feel too full. On top of that, it forces you to sit down and take time to eat (it's really hard to eat an open sandwich at the bus stop) – making it a perfect lunchtime meal for all the right reasons.

How to forage

A few years ago, Nordic food suddenly became very popular. Fancy restaurants started putting things like nettles, moss and ants on the menu, together with obscure plants that most Nordic folk had never even heard of. Along with this came a desire to get back to real foraging. We grabbed this idea by the horns and rode the wave. Of course, we all go foraging: we are the Vikings, the foragers. We live off the land. We *are* at one with the land.

To be fair, we have always liked going into nature to look for stuff we can eat. Mostly, though, until the Nordic Food Revolution, this extended to mushrooms, that wild blackberry bush by the side of the road and wild strawberries while holidaying in our cottage by the lake. And Mr Jensen's apple tree, surely that's a form of foraging, too? Aside from this, most Nordic folk didn't actually forage that much – or at least they didn't until the rest of the world started to. City-based Danes, especially the fashionable ones, can now be found wandering around suburban patches of land looking for stuff to eat.

In recent decades living off the land had become mostly about the comfort of knowing 7-Eleven had the stuff you needed late at night. Scandinavians are as much a bunch of convenience creatures as the next, and our knowledge of gathering food is as basic as most people's. We moved to the cities and we forgot how to forage; we didn't eat nettle soup and most people had never made a jar of jam in their entire lives. By and large, even today, if you send most Nordic folk into the forest on a survival course without their smartphone for fact-checking, they'd eat the wrong mushrooms and die a slow death.

That's not to say that it isn't in our genes. This pride in the Scandinavian lands has grown from a fashionable food fad and we're reconnecting, finding that we're not too bad at it, either. From a change in eating trends, our heritage and love of how things used to be done has regrown. It has been a beautiful journey, reconnecting with our food cultures and shunning the fast-food pressures that had started taking their toll on the popularity of traditional Scandinavian food and dishes – not to mention waistlines.

Foraging in Scandinavia is no different to foraging anywhere else. First, no one is going to tell you where the good patches are, because that's rule number one of foraging: never tell anyone anything. Research is essential, as is making really good friends with local foragers.

Fredagsmys

Across Scandinavia, Friday nights are important because this is when we get together as family and friends, cosy up with food, snacks and maybe a good movie. The name for this is *Fredagsmys* – in Sweden, at least. *Fredag* is the word for Friday and *mys* is the Swedish version of *hygge*, and in Norwegian it is *kos*. Replace the words accordingly, depending on the country, it is *Fredagsmys*, *Fredagskos* or *Fredagshygge*.

One of the essential foods for Friday evenings in Sweden and Norway is the taco. Tex-Mex in Scandinavian is simply known collectively as tacos. It doesn't matter if it's burritos, nachos, salsa, fajitas, soft- or hard-shell tacos. All are simply referred to as tacos. Taco Friday is one of those curious things where marketing worked so well that it changed the whole culture. Initially invented by a Tex-Mex food brand, Scandinavians took this delightful, easy-to-make food to heart in the early nineties when pre-mixed spices and ready-to-fill shells and tortillas first landed in the supermarkets. Easy to prepare at home – even children can help out – and a food that you could easily adapt to make your own. All Scandinavians add cucumbers to tacos, for an unknown reason. Ask a Scandinavian about this and they will not think it is strange at all, so your argument will last as long as it takes them to add olives. And a slice of ham. 'Add what you want' was a factor that made the food instantly popular, and by 2011, in Sweden alone the market was worth 2.1 billion Swedish krona.

Behind all of this is the essential part of Scandinavian family life: the desire to bring people we love together, sharing in comfort and unity, food and happy feelings – and, of course, letting go of the worries of the week and setting ourselves up for the weekend.

Lördagsgodis

One thing many foreigners find amusing when they get to Scandinavia is the notion of Saturday Sweets. Known as *Lördagsgodis/Lørdagsslik*), many kids are only allowed sweets on Saturdays. It also follows on very well from Cosy Friday, when they overindulge in savouries. On Saturday, it is the weekly allowance of sweet things.

While, of course, many kids only get treats on Saturdays the world over, perhaps in Scandinavia these rules have been the norm as people have grown up. For this reason, the term *Lördagsgodis* is one that makes most Scandinavians, even adults, feel very excited and rush out to buy a bag of pick 'n' mix. Swedes alone eat 17 kg (37½ lb) of sweets per person per year. Any word that can stir up emotions of togetherness in a Scandi person is always a good thing. And *Lördagsgodis* is one of those. Even if you're not a kid.

How to slice cheese

Cheese is of the upmost importance to all Scandinavians. Even if you do not eat cheese, you will be around people who consume a lot of it, so it is important to understand our love affair with what is, essentially, a bacterial process.

From the time of the Vikings, Scandinavians have been making cheese and consuming it on a grand scale. They eat 19–24 kg (42–53 lb) of cheese per person per year – in contrast to the UK, where people eat around 11.8 kg (26 lb). The quantities vary slightly year on year, but regardless, we're talking serious tyrophile stats.

In Norway, the most favoured cheese is called *brunost*, which means 'brown cheese', and it is indeed very brown. It looks a bit like plasticine and feels like it, too. Made from goats' milk that has been boiled, caramelising the milk sugars and thus turning it brown, it has a delicious, almost sweet, taste of caramel and goats: caramel goats' cheese. It's a particular taste that you either love or hate. Once you are stuck on it, you won't be able to stop eating it.

The Danes favour more pungent cows' milk cheeses, of slightly softer texture. Some of them smell like things that have gone off and have names such as *Gamle Ole* ('Old Ole'), which is a fair description of the smell (the taste is far milder, as with most Danish smellies). Only the Norwegians have a stronger cheese – an old Viking-style cheese called *Gamalost* ('really old cheese'), known to be so smelly it makes grown men cry.

Swedes like to think of themselves as the kings of cheese in Scandinavia, as they consume the most. Their cheeses range from the undisputed *Västerbotten* gourmet cheese to the more elaborately named *Hushållsost* ('household cheese').

Cheese in Scandinavia is often eaten with jam. This is a perfectly reasonable accompaniment to all kinds of cheese. Simply add butter to bread, a thick slice of your favourite cheese and a good dollop of jam on top and you have a great *mellanmål* ('afternoon snack').

In Scandinavia it is sold in very large packs, usually over 500 g–1 kg (1–2 lb) in size. This is because all cheese lives on a plate in the fridge once opened, covered in clingfilm or a plastic shower cap (it does the job in a very practical way, don't knock it) and is taken out at most morning and midday meals. Most households only have one or two cheeses on the go at any one time, which can make a Scandi cheeseboard a bit boring at times.

Next to the cheese is a slicer. There are rules one must follow when slicing cheese in Scandinavia, the first being choose your slicer carefully. If the cheese is hard, you must use a metal planer. When the cheese is slightly softer, a plastic planer will do the best job. For a lot of Danish cheeses you need a cheese slicer with string, or you end up with wonky pieces. Don't ever, ever think of simply picking up a knife to slice the cheese; just put that knife down.

Once you have chosen your appropriate equipment, make sure you slice from the correct side. The aim is not to create any sort of slope whatsoever on the cheese. These slopes, created by careless, non-trained, usually non-Scandinavian people are referred to as *skidbacke* ('ski slopes') and are considered a waste of cheese. If you cut the cheese wrong at someone's house, do not expect to be spared a snide comment even if you were introduced to your Swedish girlfriend's granddad only fifteen minutes earlier. So, instead, look at the cheese and slice from the side that is currently tallest, ensuring you help to even out the cheese to perfection. Get yourself a large block of cheese and some slicers and practise at home while simultaneously doubling your annual cheese intake in preparation for living a life more Scandinavian.

How to smörgåsbord

The word *smörgåsbord* comes from the Swedish word *smörgås*, meaning 'open sandwich' or 'buttered bread', and *bord*, meaning 'table'. Translated, it basically means a buffet made up of many smaller dishes: 'a laid-out table'. Actually, literally translated, it can mean 'butter goose table', but let's stick with 'sandwich table'.

The traditional *smörgåsbord* is slightly different, depending on the country you are in. Just follow the guidelines of what to eat and in what order and you'll be all right, no matter where you are.

The term *smörgåsbord* first cropped up outside Scandinavia during the 1939 World's Fair in New York, when a Swedish restaurant served *smörgåsbord* as it's known today. The history of *smörgåsbord*, however, goes back many centuries earlier, when it was known as 'aquavit table'. A few hours prior to dinner, shots of aquavit were served. These were accompanied by a selection of cheeses, pickles and meats laid out on a side-table to snack on before the main meal. Over the years, the choice of dishes expanded and, eventually, everything moved onto the main dinner table and thus *smörgåsbord* was born.

The essence of a real *smörgåsbord* is about taking your time to eat. There is lots of food, granted, but we tend to spend many hours eating it. No *smörgåsbord* ever took an hour – there is no time limit. It is about taking the time to enjoy small portions of lots of different things and is always done in 'rounds', so no one ever piles up their plate. You can always spot a rookie. Rookies will fill a plate like they are at an all-you-can-eat buffet. They will also hit the aquavit hard – and no rookie will last till the end.

The biggest *smörgåsbord* of the year is at Christmas. This is the *julbord* (literally meaning 'Christmas table') and is also the one that takes the longest to complete. There are many rounds and there will absolutely be beer and aquavit, too. And singing. During December, people across Scandinavia will attend many different *julbords* – there is the work *julbord*, the friends' *julbord*, the *julbord* for the golf club, the book club ... The most intimate one is always on Christmas Eve with the family. Then there is the *smörgåsbord* at Easter, Midsummer and birthdays. These are no less elaborate when celebrating at home, but there are less club and work ones to attend.

The dishes on a Scandinavian *smörgåsbord* can vary seasonally and indeed regionally, but the main dishes are the same. Always start with the herring – it is a strong fish and therefore needs its own plate and it needs aquavit too. From this follows other fish, sliced meats, warm meats, salads and other warm dishes, then cheese and then – finally – dessert. And coffee.

Everything is served buffet style or passed around the table in small servings. You will never find pre-made open sandwiches on a *smörgåsbord* – you are supposed to make your own – and you will also never find many 'fillers', such as warm potatoes or gravy (it is not a dinner, it is a cold table with a few contradictory warm dishes included).

A good old *smörgåsbord* may sound a little complicated at first, but it is a very enjoyable way to spend four–six hours with some really nice people you get along with. While Scandinavians will never, ever talk to you at the bus stop or in the supermarket, once you have sung a few merry tunes around the *smörgåsbord*, you'll be making new friends in no time. *Smörgåsbord* really is where Scandinavians open up the most and where you find our joy of the big, shared, happy table crammed with delicious food.

The basic order of the *smörgåsbord*

Whether you are in Denmark, Sweden or Norway, *smörgåsbord* is eaten in a certain order. In Sweden and Norway, all dishes are laid out at the beginning, but you still pretty much adhere to the order at casual family gatherings, less so in formal restaurants. In Denmark, dishes are mostly served at the main table and brought out one after the other. The food on the table is not cleared until towards the end, before the cheese is served.

Round one: Pickled herring (a few different kinds, served in bowls) and shots of ice-cold aquavit. Singing at this point is optional. Beer is the traditional drink served with *smörgåsbord* – it works better with aquavit than, say, wine, which just gets you even more drunk. If you do drink wine with it, take it easy, as it doesn't mix that well.

Round two: Fish and seafood dishes. Here, serve bowls of prawns, smoked mackerel, *skagenröra*, halves of hardboiled eggs or any fish other than herring – even small, warm fried plaice fillets.

Round three: Cold meats and pâté. Smoked ham, salami, liver pâté, cold roast beef, rolled sausage – any deli meats are served in this round, along with pickles and/or toppings.

Round four: Warm meats. Meatballs, roast pork, mini sausages – anything warm is served for this course. If you want to serve *Janssons frestelse* (Jansson's Temptation – a traditional Swedish gratin-style casserole made with potatoes, onions, cream and sweet pickled sprats) for the *smörgåsbord*, this is the course to do it. In summer always provide a light potato salad. Any warm sides, such as red cabbage, can be served here.

Round five: Cheese selection. Optional decorative grapes that nobody will eat and maybe a slice of green pepper.

Round six: Dessert and coffee. Any soft cake, such as a strawberry Midsummer cake or a layer cake, works here and a nice selection of little *fika* treats goes well too – there won't be many hungry people at the end of a *smörgåsbord*.

Alongside: Rye, crusty bread and crispbreads, bowls of salads (beetroot, mainly), pickles, condiments, sauces such as dill and mustard sauce, Danish remoulade and more.

Traditional drinks for *smörgåsbord*: Beer and aquavit.

How to drink aquavit

Anyone who has ever been to a traditional Scandinavian lunch will be familiar with the Scandinavian drink aquavit. Produced in Scandinavia since the fifteenth century, traditionally it is a light-coloured spirit made from grain or potato and flavoured with lots of herbs – the main ones being caraway and dill. It is usually 37.5 per cent ABV, so it is strong stuff. Lots of different herbs and spices can be used, some with a strong aniseed flavour, so it is advisable to have a few tasters to find one you like.

You usually find aquavit at a big lunchtime *smörgåsbord* or crayfish party. The host will keep a few bottles very cold and ready to serve. Most aquavit – apart from some of

the Norwegian ones – is best served ice-cold in small aquavit glasses. The usual serving is around 25–30 ml (1–1½ fl oz). Some people like their drink extra-cold and put both the aquavit and the glasses in the freezer before serving.

The most common time to start the aquavit is at the beginning of the *smörgåsbord*, when the pickled herring is served. Aquavit goes very well with herring; the flavours almost cancel each other out as well as complementing one another. At crayfish parties, the aquavit starts at the beginning of the party and stops when the bottle is empty. At Christmas, people carry on until they forget their own name and, at times, their address, which annoys taxi drivers all over Scandinavia in December.

To drink aquavit, you first allow the host to pour you a shot. You do not, ever, help yourself (bearing in mind the price of alcohol in Scandinavia). Once everybody around the table has been served, you wait for the host to say '*skål*' ('cheers'). At this point, you pick up the full glass and hold it in front of you; you do not drink it. Look at everybody: they will be trying to get eye contact with you because you have to look at everybody around the table before drinking.

Now is the tricky moment where there may or may not be singing. If in Sweden, it is likely you will now sing the song '*Helan går*', but if in Denmark, they might just want to get to the drinking bit. Follow the lead of the others. After any singing, you once again keep the full glass in front of you. Everybody will then – at the same time – drink the shot in one. Try not to make a face at this point and don't worry, you will get the feeling back in your eyeballs a moment or two later. If you wish, you can drink half.

Aquavit is one of those things that can loosen up the hardest soul. Most quiet Vikings come out of their shells after a few of these and, even if you are at a lunch where nobody knows anyone, after some aquavit you will make a bunch of new friends. It is the anti-freeze to our Scandi souls.

The point to note, however, is that aquavit tends to affect most people from the waist down. You will be fine for three or four of these little *nubbar* (as the shots are called), but once it is time to visit the 'facilities', you may find that your feet have simply stopped communicating with your brain. It takes concentration to win that power back. Rest assured, you will not be the only one. *Skål*!

How to breakfast

The main event

Scandinavians don't tend to skip breakfast. First, the fuel is needed to brave the outdoors and, second, there's the coffee need. We rarely and barely function without it. What is quickly evident is the lack of focus on refined sugars at the breakfast table, instead breakfast is a little bit of sweet and a little bit of savoury.

The dairy part

The Nordic people enjoy a centuries-long love affair with dairy products. We love drinking milk and we also love it when it goes sour – then we call it *fil* or *afil/A38* and it's even better for our tummies. We also love Skyr, which is actually a young cheese disguised as a yoghurt.

If you're looking for the cereal ...

The Swedish term *fil och flingor* means 'soured milk and flakes', so any type of cereal, really. We love cereals and are especially fond of porridges, too – from your basic porridge to ones with added rye or ancient grains and so on.

The fruit part

Berries usually feature on the breakfast table, too. We have so many of them that, in the summer especially, you'll be served berries with quite a lot of meals. If it's not summer, then you'll have jam or compotes instead. Or defrosted berries. Or any other way that anyone could have thought of to preserve berries.

The fish part

Swedes and Norwegians can't get through the morning routine without their beloved creamed cod roe – in Sweden, the most popular of which is Kalles Kaviar, or just Kalles. It is by far the most popular morning item. While it is an acquired taste, it is easy to get used to. On crispbread add sliced, hardboiled egg and a good squeeze of the cod roe – a great way to start the day. Alternatively, add a dollop to your boiled egg and eat it like that. Once you start your day with Kalles Kaviar, you're on your way to true Swedishness.

Björns that brunch

Since breakfast is such a major ritual during the week, come the weekend Scandinavians love to go out for breakfast and in cafés all over you will find great breakfast/brunch spreads. Less of the heavy eggs Benedict, more of the platter with rye bread, fruit salad, boiled eggs, jams and cheeses – and *fil* soured milk, of course. In some places, they add a bit of bacon on the side for a real treat. Scrambled egg and salmon is very popular in Norway, where they have more than enough salmon.

In Denmark a very different tradition holds strong on the weekend: the local baker (*bageren*). Here, you will find queues of hastily dressed people who have rushed down to the baker on a Sunday morning to queue for freshly baked bread. Denmark has a long tradition of bakers and weekend mornings are the time for *rundstykker* – bread rolls. If you ever holiday in Denmark, seek out your local baker and be sure to pop by for fresh bread and pastries – it's worth the walk in your PJs. It's a real occasion for the whole family to sit down together and enjoy what we don't usually have: white bread. What a treat.

Life outside

The darkness

The Scandinavian winter is harsh on outsiders. Think snow, ice, more snow, storms, utter darkness… To be honest, that's only really up north. There is a lot of weather difference between Svalbard and Malmö. That being said, from around October until March, things are pretty bleak, even in the south. Some may think it is tough to be all the way up in the north, but actually, at times, the sleet and constant grey of Copenhagen aren't much fun either. With everything smothered in some sort of permanent dark hue, Scandinavians have had to find ways to cope. Winter is long when it lasts five months, no matter what angle you look at it. Still, there are a few things you can do to get through it:

Acceptance

Step one is accepting there will be no daylight to speak of. When it is not dark, it's grey. Worse still, it may also rain (horizontally, if you are in Gothenburg). Snow is not so bad, because snow reflects and it lights up the sky a bit. The real downer is the sleet and rain. Knowing in advance it will be dark means you can prevent the winter sadness setting in. The symptoms are fatigue, lethargy, depression and not wanting to do anything, least of all to be with other people. This may be ok in a place where you have a month or so of darkness, but if you spend five months like that, it's a waste of time. So, accept it – and make a plan.

Pull together

There's something about safety in numbers. Make plans to occupy those evenings, not just spending them alone. Even if it's dark outside, go do stuff, just for an hour or so. Go on a course in abstract art or learn to play the tuba. Anything. We're all in this together and it's fine to discuss the weather for about an hour a day – it really helps.

Get outside

Now that you have accepted months of grey and darkness, make plans to get out into it. Plan your weekends around long walks, hikes and – if there's no ice – maybe some good bike rides. Go for snow runs or just runs in the forest or around the lakes. Play sports. Move your body. Walk to work, even if it's dark. Take a walk in your lunch break. Make sure you don't stop going to the gym or doing yoga – all of these things help release good feelings in your body and brain and will carry you through the dark times. A good, brisk walk will energise you beyond belief if you are feeling down. Scandinavians spend a lot of time outdoors all year round, even in the winter.

Lights

To get through winter, make sure you get enough exposure to sunlight. Use your weekend daylight hours – don't waste them – and make sure you take a lunch break during the week and get outside. Unless you have a SAD lamp in your office (they work too), the best medicine is just to be in the sun for a little while and top up your daylight levels.

Cosy up

At home, candles. And lots of small lamps everywhere to create that all-important atmosphere of *hygge*. Create your hibernation space with stuff that makes you happy. You can practise your tuba here, if you want to. Or watch re-runs of *Wallander*, spend time with the family, eat good food and be nice to your stress levels by going to bed early once in a while.

Eat good stuff

When feeling low and in the darkness, it is easy to reach for the crisps and the sugar. If you are Scandinavian, you will only do this on Friday evenings and on Saturdays, so try to eat well the other days of the week. As there is not much in terms of fresh local produce around, stick to the good staples and lots of smoked and pickled fish and veg.

Set milestones

If Halloween marks the start of the winter, let Christmas be the first milestone you look towards. It's so full of light and *hygge* feelings, it is impossible not to be drawn into the excitement of it all. After Christmas, look towards the Lent season, full of cream cakes. Then it's Easter and you can look forward to the last skiing of the year. And so we're all done and it's almost Midsummer. See? It wasn't that bad, was it?

Marvel at the beauty of it all

The closed-in darkness becomes almost magical. The streetlights are on all the time and all the houses have lights outside and in the windows 24/7. Towns flicker in lights all day and all night – it is truly spectacular. Don't be scared of the dark, because after dark, comes light. And in darkness, all light burns that much brighter and stronger. Scandinavian winter is a gentle giant that will carry you through, if you let it.

The never-ending daytime

In contrast to the total darkness, never having the sun set may seem like a wonderful thing. Well, it is, sort of. It's nice to have light and green but other things start to happen to your head that perhaps you would not expect.

From Land of Always Winter comes Land of Midnight Sun. The further north you are, the bigger the extreme between winter darkness and summer light. Most Scandinavians don't feel any extreme – you need to be north of Oslo to notice the bigger differences. Most people feel like the eternal day messes up their internal clock (known as the circadian rhythm), as exposure to daylight automatically makes us perk up. It's like when you used to go out clubbing, come home at 7 a.m. and try desperately to get to sleep, with the sun glaring outside. Impossible. Getting to sleep is another issue. While most adults can learn to do it, spare a thought for the parents of young children who will inevitably spend much of the summer up most of the night, thinking it's daytime ergo playtime.

The thing that regulates our sleep is the production of a hormone called melatonin. It increases at night and decreases during the day. If you get light exposure later on in the day, it can stall the melatonin release, so you don't feel tired. So, naturally, people who live up north will sleep less in the summer than they do in the winter – and you may find them building a tool shed or doing some gardening at 10 p.m. It's the opposite in winter, when we naturally feel more sluggish and tired.

In contrast to the acceptance of the Gentle Giant of Winter, try to appreciate the fact that you can take advantage of daylight that never ends. Summer insomnia at 3 a.m. means you

can actually just get on with stuff (although you do have to be dedicated to getting some sleep or things really will start to wobble). There are many positive things about a lot of daylight. Need to do a bit of sightseeing? Don't rush, it won't get dark anyway. Need to go for a run? You can do it at 11 p.m. without the need for a head torch. Endless summers also means you have loads of time to enjoy the outdoors. Your body, if you move it enough, will regulate itself and you will be able to sleep because you are physically tired.

Having a clearly set schedule will help. Make sure you go to bed at the same time and wake up at the same time every day, without too much deviation. This will also help if you have young children, who then will not have parties at 2 a.m. Save those for the teenage years and marvel at the effectiveness of strict learnt patterns that will, usually, override the natural urge to stay up. These set schedules should include drawing the curtains at least an hour before bedtime, avoid stimulation of screens and caffeine, etc. and just allowing yourself to feel calm.

For the people far up near the Arctic Circle, where these extreme seasons of light and dark are a reality and not a novelty, they will tell you that the darkness is tougher than the light. The lack of natural vitamin D takes its toll and you have to work harder at not going into social hibernation. On the flipside, they will tell you that the summer months, in contrast, make you feel incredibly alive. However, to be able to appreciate either fully, you have to live through them both. So best pack those bags; see you in a year or so.

Ut på tur (hiking in Norway)

There is a Norwegian saying that goes *'Ut på tur, aldri sur!'*, which means 'Out on tour, never sour!' You should never start your hike in a mood. Sing this merry little tune in your head every time you head out for a hike, especially if you are not in the frame of mind to be out walking.

Norwegians' love of hiking and skiing is second to none. Weekends and holidays are spent getting out into the fresh air and heading upwards to a hill or mountain, on foot or skis. To *gå på tur* ('go for a walk') is a favourite pastime – and is done by everybody.

If it's Sunday and impractical for you to get out of the city, you are allowed to take your walk in parks and around where you live. These are leisurely walks, but do not include popping to the shops for a pint of milk: the walk has to be for the purpose of the walk itself. During a *Søndagstur* (Sunday walk), you should factor in a stop for coffee. You must also bring one treat – usually a chocolate bar – and, if there is any kind of snow or ice, an orange. Refreshing and completely impractical to peel when your fingers are frozen, nevertheless essential. (The word *Søndagstur* can also be used in Norwegian to describe something that was easy, as in 'How was that half marathon yesterday?' 'Like a *Søndagstur*.')

For more strenuous day-long hikes, appropriate equipment is essential, including physical maps, because you are unlikely to have any phone reception. Half of Norway is made up of mountains, the rest is fjords, rivers and lakes. Very little of the land is urbanised and it's a huge place – about the same size as the UK and Ireland put together but with only 4.6 million people to populate it. It's no wonder you can go out on a hike and see nobody for days and days, so best to be prepared like a native or risk getting lost.

For these longer hikes, still bring the obligatory orange, your Kvikk Lunsj chocolate bar (although other brands are allowed) and a thermos of coffee. Top it off with that all-important Norwegian hiking smile. Do remember that out on hikes is the only time that the rule of not talking to strangers is not applicable; when you see others out on a hike, you must greet them and smile, as you hurry past on your leisure hike.

When hiking properly, also make sure you bring plasters and wear really good shoes. The kind that give you serious blisters for the first few months (hence the plasters). Eventually, after some twenty-seven hikes, you'll wear the shoes in, won't get blisters, and you'll never want to buy new shoes unless you absolutely have to. Dress for the weather. Don't try to get away without layering. Wear proper waterproofs if it's raining. Norwegians out hiking tend to look like an advert for comfortable hiking clothes (in rather bright colours). To recap: smile, comfy clothes, maps, hot beverage, chocolate, orange. Happy hiking!

Barbecue like a Scandinavian

Barbecuing in Scandinavia is a serious business. Not quite like barbecuing in other countries where sun is a prevailing factor for a successful event. Scandinavians have adapted the notion of barbecue to be an all-year thing. More: me Viking, me Viking cooking over real fire. Sod the rain.

In Sweden, most 'out in the open' (*friluft*) sport pursuits factor in some form of barbecuing. All ski resorts have communal barbecue pits where families can huddle, like cold penguins, around smouldering coal in -20°C (-4°F). Here, only sausages are cooked, rarely anything else, as people can't move their fingers. You put the half-burnt wieners in a cold bun and feel the singe as the skin on the left side of your mouth melts away, while the other side of the sausage is still cold. It is likely to be the best hotdog you have ever had.

In Norway, you will also find many barbecue spots when out hiking. This is an open invitation to talk to people you don't know, a practice forbidden unless you are out and about *being one* with nature.

Danes don't barbecue in winter. First, there is never really enough snow to make a go of it and they have the warmest summers of all the three countries and can therefore be allowed to be a bit continental about the whole barbecuing season.

When not grilling fancy cuts of meat at home, Danes do like to bake on an open fire. Most often, at Midsummer, they like to make 'stick bread' (*snobrød*). This is a peculiar Scouts' invention of wrapping bread dough around a long wooden stick (ideally cut from a nearby tree and whittled to the right shape). You then hover it just above the smouldering embers until it is cooked on the outside, then fill to the brim with jam or a hotdog sausage. The inside is usually still raw and all children end up with stomach aches, but at least they have been cooking outside.

All Scandinavians have been brought up knowing there is no such thing as bad weather, only bad clothing. This is why, during the summer months, many people can often be found sitting in their gardens in the rain under umbrellas, eating charred food. Dad standing by the new barbecue, umbrella in hand, mumbling obscenities to himself, but secretly proud of being at one with nature. We'll be damned if we'll ever let the weather beat our plans for a good family dinner.

Favourite sports

Nordic people love sports – we are sporty people. Admittedly, we're better at some than others and some sports we've decided not even to bother with. Nordic people also have a deep love of the outdoors. Come rain, shine, snow, sleet, more snow, we will still make it outside and feel our cheeks go a healthy red colour. It's simply a bonus if we get to move around inside or out so we can burn off all those *fika* calories. In fact, we love every kind of weather, except heat, when we come up with error messages. Wherever you go in Scandinavia, you will find people who love the outdoors and combine it with activities. From flat walks and cycling in Denmark and the occasional football win to serious day hikers all over the northern parts, the outdoors and sport are where it's at. In all kinds of weather, for every kind of person, there is a sporty pursuit to be had. Just get off that sofa.

Fodbold (D) */ fotball* (N) */ fotboll* (S)

We like it a lot and it's part of every kid's upbringing across Scandinavia. Sometimes, one of the countries qualifies for the World or European Championship. This causes excitement beyond belief to ripple through the nations. If Denmark and Sweden happen to meet in a group, and a draw is enough for them both to get through, Denmark will offer Sweden the island of Bornholm in exchange for a pre-arranged draw. Sweden never officially accepts, but it is currently owed around seven Bornholm islands because of draws in the final scores. As if football could be pre-arranged, like Eurovision. Not that we pre-arrange anything, of course, that would be cheating; it just happened to be that way (sorry, Italy, for Euro 2004, we feel really bad about that. By the way, try Bornholm for your next holiday, it's a lovely place).

Our footballers never look that glamorous when they play, but they are usually pretty solid performers. Scandinavian players are like your good mates from back home: the ones who will never leave you, but only a few make it out of the village while the rest stay behind. We have had a few good ones over the years.

If several Nordic nations happen to qualify for a championship, each Nordic nation will support only their own team. If there is only one country left, it is possible each will support the other Nordic nations, except if it's Denmark or Sweden. Danes will never support Sweden or vice versa. Norway has never got that far so it has never been an issue to consider.

In 1992, Denmark didn't qualify for the European championship in Sweden and were resigned to staying at home. Then Yugoslavia pulled out at the last minute because of the war and, suddenly, there was a chance. No one counted on anything and Denmark went all the way through to the final against Germany. They won and there was a party for many days in Copenhagen – a party only equalled when they won Eurovision a few years later. Never underestimate the Scandi underdog – although Denmark hasn't won anything since, so they still talk about 1992 every time anyone will listen.

Håndbold (D)/håndboll (N)/handboll (S)

We're really, really good at this. Mainly because only we – along with a few other countries – play it and nobody else bothers, so we can be particularly good at it quite easily. It's a good sport for us because we can do it indoors all year, doubling our training possibilities.

Handball in Scandinavia is almost as popular as football. Most kids play handball at school and, at a competitive level, both women's and men's teams are extremely popular and big matches are televised, with huge viewing figures.

Two teams of seven players each (six outfield players and a goalkeeper) pass a ball using their hands with the aim of throwing it into the goal of the other team. A standard match consists of two periods of thirty minutes, and the team that scores the most goals wins. The game is fast-paced with lots of goals – it is not unusual to have twenty or thirty goals in a game.

Ishockey

Swedes in particular are really good at ice hockey. Finns too. It is not that popular in Norway or Denmark, but Sweden and Finland have national leagues and also play internationally.

Two teams play – there are six on each team (one goalkeeper and five others). There are lots of people on the bench and unlimited substitutions. It is played on ice, on skates, in full protective gear. There are three time periods, each twenty minutes in length, and the objective is to get the puck into the other team's goal.

Bandy is a similar game in that it is played on ice and very popular in Norway and Sweden. There are eleven skaters on the team and it is a game of two halves, each of forty-five minutes. In essence, it is a bit like football on ice, except with smaller balls.

Stavgang (D)/Ståvgang (S)

We're also really good at walking. So good, in fact, we made a sport out of it and now you can walk like a Nordic, because you do this with poles. In Scandinavia, Nordic Walking is just known as walking or hiking, we don't need to call it Nordic. In some places it is also referred to as pole-walking. You simply walk with your poles. For a long time. Whole days, even. You push the stride with your poles, which means you get a full-body workout. It is a good way for people of all athletic abilities to exercise – and it can be very sociable, too, as you can still manage to carry on talking. Norwegians and Swedes are especially good at it because they are already good at cross-country skiing. In Denmark, people also love

walking, but the lack of any sort of hills means there is little use for the poles to help you along. So there, it's more like, well, just walking.

Nordic cold yoga

This does not exist, but we're working on it. It could be a thing: Frozen Yoga. Someone should really invent that.

Viking Method Workout (*Berserk*)

This is a real thing that promises to turn you into your chosen Thor, Freya or Baldur. Devised by Icelandic trainers, it promises a no-nonsense method of pure training. The website says 'not for the looks, but the look is a by-product'. It consists of core training, of timed anaerobic and aerobic resistance training, which is done using your body weight – and, of course, it's all high intensity. You will be out in the snow, the rain, early and late, *and there will be NO EXCUSES*. In short, it's a method you'd think was developed by Thor himself.

Curling

The Canadians taught us about curling and we're nifty with a brush and we're good on ice. Norwegians are especially good at it, but it is quite a popular sport all over Scandinavia. It is hard to look cool when you do curling, but Scandinavians give it a go. The Norwegian team usually sports an 'interesting' outfit when they compete, which does make the whole thing more exciting to watch.

Golf

Golf is popular in Scandinavia, like it is everywhere. There is a lot of space to play on, so there are many golf courses and you do not need to be rich to afford membership. We have even produced quite a few international golf players.

FEIL VEI–SNU!
WRONG WAY
TURN AROUND!

Skiing

All Scandinavian people, except the Danes, ski from a young age. In Norway especially, there is no option but to get out there on your baby skis and learn to navigate the snow. To a Norwegian, being able to ski is simply second nature. Swedes follow a close second. For centuries, the people in the Northern shores have skied. There is even a god of skiing, called Ullr, in Norse mythology.

Every winter, Norwegians and Swedes go to their cottages up north and do cross-country or downhill skiing. Danes also quite like going up there for skiing, but they are less adept at it. Some Norwegians do the 54-kilometre (33½-mile) Birkebeiner race across mountains. In Sweden, there is the 90-kilometre (56-mile) Vasaloppet ski race. Why do small runs when you can ski like Ullr?

Norway wins everything

Norway wins the Winter Olympics every year; it's a wonder anyone else bothers taking part. Usually topping the medals tables, they have won 329 medals since starting to take part in 1924. Sweden is also pretty good, with 144 medals in the Winter Olympics. Denmark is rubbish, with only one medal won in any Winter Olympics, ever. And that was in curling.

How to bicycle

Getting on your bike is big in Denmark. Everyone does it, all the time. While people in other Scandinavian places also love their bikes, nobody loves them quite as much as the Danes do. It's not a new thing, this love of bikes, which is why they have always ensured sufficient space for cycling. Copenhagen got its first bike lane in 1892, when there were only a few bikes – and cars – around. Good forward thinking in the planning department, because today half a million new bikes are sold each year in a country of just five million people. To a Dane, bikes are how you get around in the most efficient way in terms of time, flexibility and cost.

Most cities have carefully planned-out bike lanes, safe from cars – in fact, there are over 12,000 kilometres (75,450 miles) of signposted bike routes across the country. In Copenhagen alone, more people use a bike to get to work than use a car or public transport. In fact, most trips are less than 5 kilometres (3 miles) long, making the bike the perfect mode of transport, while providing exercise.

Children in Denmark are on their bikes from an early age – around three years old – and, after a few years, they will cycle along the bike lanes. Almost half of kids bike to school, with plenty of provision for them to get there safely. In 1984, the first Christiania Bike was made. The concept caught on and these bikes are now sold across the world as Copenhagen bikes. A Christiania Bike is a bike with a box on the front, perfect for transporting your young children to and from nursery. It can also be used for shopping, lazy dogs and getting drunk friends home from the pub.

As a pedestrian in big cities, it is important to learn how not to get injured by cyclists. The bike lanes are their domain and they whizz through these, fast and determined. Look before you cross a bike lane, because you won't hear cyclists before they get to you. And they *will* run you over: this is the land where bikes rule, make no mistake.

Helmet use is a bit controversial. While everybody knows that helmets protect your head in case of a fall, not many Danish adults wear them (despite it not being a legal requirement, 75 per cent of younger kids do wear them). Interestingly, despite their attitude to helmets, statistics show proportionally there are fewer accidents in countries where people cycle a lot (the Netherlands, Denmark, Germany and Hungary, to name a few), perhaps because the consideration for cyclists is so high in the first place.

Getting on your bike in Denmark is simple – have a little study online of the basic dos and don'ts, get yourself a big bike and off you go.

How to sauna

'*Saunassa ollaan kuin kirkossa*' ('In the sauna one must conduct oneself as one would in church') – Finnish saying.

The word sauna comes from the Finnish, who have built sweat rooms since the Middle Ages. Over time sweat rooms became lodges and eventually became the sauna we know today.

A sauna is a small room, usually wooden, with dry heat that encourages perspiration and hot stones with water that increase humidity. The sauna cleanses you through perspiration and, because of the heat, is a very clean place, which also explains why it was traditionally used as a birthing place.

All over the world, a sauna is called a sauna, because 'sweat room' doesn't sound nice. Except in Sweden and Norway, where it is called a *bastu* (which originally meant 'bath house'). Nobody is sure why Sweden and Norway are the only countries not to adopt the word sauna, although if you use it, they will know what you mean.

Saunas are popular across all of the Nordic countries and have largely escaped the seedy reputation that they sometimes have in other places. In the Nordics, the sauna is a place for friends and family and for rejuvenation and cleanliness.

A good sauna session has a temperature of 70–100°C (158–212°F). The higher end of this scale is reserved for the experts, whereas normal people feel most enjoyment at 70–90°C (158–194°F). The reason people can stand the heat is because the humidity is controlled. The high temperature promotes good sweating, so you perspire and cleanse yourself. You can slow-cook a beef roast when the oven is at 80°C (176°F) – remember that when considering staying in the sauna a bit longer.

In Finland, they used to have championships in which people competed to stay in the sauna the longest. It was not a pretty competition as it involved very sweaty men wearing extremely small Speedos. These competitions stopped in 2010 after one of the contestants died.

The best thing to wear in a dry sauna is your birthday suit. That way, you are unlikely to stand out, as most others will be wearing the same. If you feel a bit funny about having your bits on show, you can keep a towel wrapped around you. Most public saunas tend to be families together, then one for males and one for females; some are mixed. Sometimes, in the mixed ones, people keep their swimmers on because they tend to be near the pool. In short, look around: if people are naked around you, do the same. Either way, you don't want to be the odd one out. Always bring your towel to sit on, though, or else it's considered unclean. Nobody wants to see the imprint of your sweaty bum on the seat when you leave.

Nordic people, in general, don't really have an issue with the human body. It's just skin; it really isn't a big deal and we find it odd that others think nudity is so hilarious. Sauna is a health activity; it is good for you and no one considers it a sexual thing any more than we do going to the supermarket. Note: we only go to the supermarket fully clothed.

At lakeside saunas or in ski resorts, it is not unusual for the saunas to be mixed. It is also quite normal to run out and plunge into cold water – or even roll around in the snow, if you really feel like it. An *isvak* in Swedish is a hole in the ice on the lake. A quick dip after a hot sauna will make you remember all the reasons why you are alive – and is worth trying if you ever get the chance.

When going to a sauna, always shower first. If you want to put water on the stones to increase the heat and humidity, there are no hard and fast rules on when to do this, but do look around and grunt at the people who are in the sauna with you, just to check it is ok to go ahead. It's fine to chat in a sauna, although do always bear in mind that Scandinavians don't talk to people they don't know. Ever. Whether naked or not, talking to strangers isn't the done thing – so usually, unless you are with friends, accept that your *bastu*-time is one of contemplation, calm and quiet.

Family life

How to ... date a Scandinavian

First, you need to know that dating isn't really a thing. And now, in the days of Tinder, even less so because the rules are always changing. Second, the Scandinavian behavioural codes differ slightly. Those little cultural differences, from each of the three countries, come into play much more when you spend that time with someone, getting to know them in a more intimate and romantic way. Let's pretend we're in the pre-Tinder era and you are actually looking to hook up with someone in the more old-fashioned way, less swiping left and right. Here's a short guide to the big stuff:

We don't date

Of course, we have watched the movies and we know how it's done, so it is likely your new love interest will humour you and go on a date. Sure, it's nice to have someone open the door or take you to dinner, but those are the exception rather than the norm. There are no big-pressure first dates. Dating is parading, not getting to know someone. It's not what is usually done – unless you meet for a *fika* date, in which case, it is just coffee and nobody needs to have their hair done.

We don't talk to strangers

Ever tried to talk to a Scandi person at a bus stop? That will give you an idea of what talking to strangers is like in any sober situation in Scandinavia. It's a wonder we ever meet any new people at all, really, and we thank the heavens for the invention of strong alcohol. Actually getting a Scandinavian person to talk to you could well be hurdle number one.

Flirting isn't something we're very good at (unless we're drunk)

Both men and women in Scandinavia need some Dutch courage to flirt. We are not natural flirts. Considering the social codes say 'don't talk to strangers anywhere, ever', flirting is tough. Add alcohol. On the flipside, while we might not be good at doing it, we are reasonably good at receiving it. Be prepared to be laughed at and get a comment such as 'Wow, you're full of it!' because if you go over the top, the response will be brutal.

Dealing with the directness

If you can't deal with directness, don't go near a Scandi. It is not a rude thing, it is a cultural thing. Scandinavians in general do not beat around the bush. A spade is a spade. Your love interest will reply 'no' or 'yes' and will never add 'sorry'. No need to be sorry about it – it's a question and you got a reply. The directness should be seen as a help rather than a

hindrance. Imagine, you never have to worry about 'Does she like me?' again because she will tell you. If you cannot deal with the directness and you take offence easily, this is where you get off the train, because this relationship isn't likely to go further.

Dinner is quite a big thing

Who wants to sit there for several hours with someone they don't know and then pay for it? Awkward. Do something else instead and save the dinner for the third date. Eating in restaurants is expensive in Scandinavia, too expensive for first dates.

Split the bill

Nobody ever expects one person to pay for everything: it's all too expensive. Split the bill. If your date insists, make a judgement call. But most likely it is safer to split it half and half. Male, female, it matters not ... pay for yourself.

Everybody takes the initiative

If you like someone, take the initiative. This is completely normal, so don't be put off by any forwardness. Forwardness is direct and it lessens complications.

Sex is sex

Perhaps one of the main myths about Scandinavians is that they readily have sex with everyone. This is where some non-Scandinavians go wrong and make huge faux pas. Scandinavians are not 'easy', they are comfortable with their own bodies in general, comfortable talking about sex, about what they like and do not like. Again, directness finds the path to much pleasure in relationships with Scandinavian people. But this is not the same as 'easy' and it is incredibly offensive that other cultures view this happiness about our own sexual interests as something others can and should take advantage of. Again, no is a no and just do not – ever – cross that line.

We date exclusively

Bar a few voyeurs, most Scandinavian people don't tend to be expected to have 'the conversation' about dating exclusively. It's usually a given that it's monogamous if you are seeing someone regularly. If you are concerned whether or not this is the case, a simple 'Are we sleeping with other people?' will suffice. You will likely get a frank 'yes' or 'no' reply.

We take a long time

Scandinavians, both men and women, marry late. We take a long time to form that marrying kind of relationship. There is no 'I love you even though we only met yesterday' nonsense – everything is much more long-term and considered.

I love you

To say 'I love you' in Scandinavia is a huge thing. Massive. Actually, not said very often at all. Before 'I love you' comes *forelsket* – this means more than fancy, less than I love you. You can be *forelsket* in someone without loving them. If you just like someone, you are not *forelsket*. It's pre-love. It's being in love, but before the I love you. Confused?

How to know if it's working

Ask him or her.

How long to wait before he or she calls?

Who cares, you make the call.

How to be in a relationship

The common ground

As with any relationship, there have to be some shared values and common ground. For this reason, if you are thinking of a long-term relationship with, or of marrying, a Scandinavian, you should probably read up on your equality basics. Sure, nowhere is perfect, but Scandinavia is a very equal place all round between partners – men, women, in any combination.

Scandinavians, generally speaking, are assertive in their attitude, not afraid to speak their mind in the relationship, but usually good at talking things over and getting to a solution when there are problems. Being in touch with your feelings – and happy to discuss all of them in great detail in the relationship – is a plus. There might be tears, because Scandinavians are tough, but they also know how to show emotion. Of course, there are always exceptions to the rule and you may end up with Viking Ragnar, who isn't so much about emotion, but more about his beard.

In general, marriage is often done at a later stage, sometimes after the children come along. Nobody cares when people get married nowadays and the paperless marriages offer as much protection as marriages. Once married, people often keep their own name. Sometimes surnames can be combined or the woman's surname wins out. It is all done by discussion on what works best, not what is traditional.

Once married, your new Scandinavian spouse will likely try to implement single-duvet sleeping arrangements. Don't fear, it is perfectly normal and it doesn't mean they don't love you. Most Scandinavian couples have two single duvets on the marital bed – it is practical and it avoids duvet fights. Also, do not fear, it is normal for Scandinavians to make the bed with the duvet and blankets folded entirely on top of the bed, with nothing hanging down the sides and no excess cushions to make it look pretty. We like campbed-style beds. Simple and neat.

The wedding

Scandinavian weddings are fun, often because there is free alcohol. Even in Norway. So, naturally people drink a lot and they often drink too much and then they dance and talk to people they don't know. In Sweden, especially, speeches are extremely popular. Anyone who wants to make a speech can do so as long as they sign up with the Toastmaster during the evening. It is considered very rude to eat during a speech, which is why 1) dessert is often served at midnight and 2) people die of starvation because someone from the groom's high-school ice-hockey team decided to give a twenty-seven-minute speech at 10.32 p.m.

In Denmark, there are also speeches, but these are done alongside home-composed lyrics of questionable quality, sung by all to the tune of 'My Bonnie Lies Over The Ocean' or 'Yellow Submarine'. Danes find these songs cute, fun and traditional. Everybody else nods and has another drink.

The divorce

Around fifty per cent of marriages in Scandinavia end in divorce. Is it because they don't fight to save their marriages? Perhaps, but some of the reasons behind this are that divorce is not a stigma, nor is it a massive impact financially as both parties usually work full-time. There is less need to stay in a relationship that's no longer full of love and people move on. Even in Viking times, women could divorce their husbands – for reasons such as 'showing too much chest hair', believe it or not. Ok, they did not have traditional marriages as we do today but still, back then, women had the right to end a relationship, the same way that both parties have today.

Custody is not awarded to the mother as a given, but to both parents. If it has to go to court, the mother does not get preferential treatment and the decision is made based on equal rights as parents. It is not uncommon for kids to have a say in the matter as well.

Raising Scandi kids

Let's get one thing straight: raising your kids on Scandinavian principles doesn't make them any better behaved than any other kids and there are pluses and minuses with all parenting styles. Kids are kids. It is hard to write a guide on how to raise your kids a bit more Nordic, because we are very fortunate to have governments that support parents during the first years to be able to spend a lot of time at home and lucky because childcare is free or nearly free. Without this support, it is hard to be a 'Scandinavian parent'.

Maternity/paternity leave

Because the Scandinavian people in general believe strongly that both parents should be around, employers are helped to make this possible by generous paternity and maternity packages. Sweden tops the list with 480 days paid leave for parents. This leave can be shared between the parents, taken by both simultaneously, or used by only one parent. Either way, you have over a year to connect with your child and fully understand the art of being a Latte Dad or Latte Mum. Norway and Denmark have similar arrangements.

Let your baby sleep outside in nature

Let the little nipper sleep in his or her pram, in the snow, outside, wrapped in super-cosy clothing – but allowed to breathe the chilly fresh air. It's proven to make your child sleep really well. In Scandinavia, you often find prams parked outside cafés with the babies still in them. If you are going to do this in a place where it is not acceptable to leave your child alone outside, invest in a really warm coat, gloves and hat and park yourself outside for a few hours. Or just go for really long walks in the cold, every day. It will also help you to be outside, anyway.

Play

A Scandinavian childhood is about play. Outdoors. Lots and lots of play. Lots of outdoors. Lots of fun sports. Followed by more play. Remember, bored kids rebel and bored kids misbehave more.

Late to school

Wait until they are six or seven and expect the first few years to be lots of play learning. It is not unusual for a Scandinavian child not to be able to read until around eight years of age. If a British child gets to eight unable to read, it is likely that he or she will have special education measures, have been evaluated by a psychologist and even ear-marked as

behind. This wouldn't usually happen in a Scandinavian school until the child was older. Neither of these approaches is wrong, they are just different. The Scandinavian method allows the child to find their 'thing' later on and not feel pressured.

Schooling

In Scandinavian schools, there are no uniforms. Equality is promoted and teachers are called by their first name. It is fine to question the teacher and to expect an answer.

Often, what children eat at school are packed lunches or carefully controlled school meals. Parents by and large control what goes into a child's mouth at school and you will not find crisps or sweets in Scandinavian schools.

School in Scandinavia usually starts before 8 a.m. The school days are shorter, there is less focus on homework and many kids happily attend free after-school clubs, usually linked to the schools, which involve lots of sports and other activities. These are staffed by trained teachers and are never an afterthought, but a valued add-on to the education system overall.

Social structure and schooling

The Scandinavian education system is set up to educate and also to teach about society. No child is left behind, every child is looked after and only rarely would a kid be moved up or down a class. There are few exams, hardly any assessments until around fourteen–fifteen years old and certainly no grading of the child's abilities. Lots of outdoor time and learning through activities are encouraged.

Socially, Nordic schools set about educating the children in one big average group, with little room for high-flyers and, similarly, no room to be left behind. It means the poorer performers are helped up – but high-flyers are often under-nurtured. Primary and secondary education is broad, very broad, with little opportunity to specialise until later on. Some may view this as restrictive, but in Scandinavia, it means allowing your child to do lots of different things and make up their mind later on. How many people really knew at fourteen that they wanted to be a behavioural psychologist? In Scandinavia, jobs are, by and large, equal, but the sin is doing a job you don't enjoy.

Opinions and truth

Nordic kids are in general rather opinionated. It is part of their upbringing to be encouraged in voicing opinions, debate and general stuff that is often thought to create brats. Sometimes, you do get brats. If handled with consistency and thought, you often get well-mannered, opinionated children who will have been told the truth, mostly, when asking questions as they grow up.

The right to swear

Swearing is not ok. Not at all. But Scandinavian kids swear in English a lot – not because they are allowed to swear but because English swear words don't mean anything to them. Parents won't correct them. 'S**t' and 'f**k' are common words for young kids to use. Blame the telly, blame the internet – but don't blame the parents. It's totally normal. But if you swear in a Scandi language, expect to be scolded and sent to your room.

Parents: get home for pick-up. But don't stay home all day

Do you get home from work at 9 p.m. and only see your kids at the weekend? It's likely this bit needs to change if you are to achieve a more Scandi style of parenting. Even if you do work a lot, do you spend time with your children when you are with them? Or is every waking moment spent fitting in a tight schedule of waking, school, after-school activities, homework, tutoring Mandarin, bedtime schedule etc. – and the weekends filled with more activities? Relax and turn the speed down. Talk to your kids and ask them what they like, find out about them. Your kids will fit in around a more relaxed lifestyle better than a rigid one. Be together properly – and switch that TV off. Take a walk in the forest – it's free. *That* is the Nordic way.

Resolving conflicts

Always a sticky point for any parent. In Scandinavia, ultimatums aren't used often, because conflicts tend to be centred around 'sorting things out'. It is possible to avoid ultimatums, but only if situations are solved with empathy and learning. This is not to say Nordic kids don't have tantrums. Children will and, in some situations, you have to leave them to it. Even if it's in the supermarket. Letting a child calm down and solve a situation on his or her own teaches a lot of coping skills. Yes, it's horrid and, no, nobody likes the supermarket tantrum. But all parents have been there.

Will it make me a better parent?

No, it's likely you're doing just fine as you are. If you strive, however, to give them a childhood more like the ones of yesteryear – running around fields and playing more – then the Nordic way isn't a bad way to start. That said, there is nothing wrong with

most schools of parenting and your child will likely still grow up into a wonderful human being, compassionate and kind. Scandinavians are not deliberately smug about how we rear children – we value our way of raising kids because this fits in with the system and opportunities available to us. If you have issues with your child's behaviour, you're much better off just doing the basics instead of trying to fit into another nation's methods. These are simple first steps: play more, spend time together, talk to your kids, encourage opinions, and switch off the darn devices. Oh, also, eat proper food. Together.

Understanding the family

child/children	*barn* (S, N)/*børn* (D)
mother	*mor*/*mamma* (all)
father	*far* (D)/*fassan* (S slang) (two 's's or else it's a pheasant), *pappa* (N, S)
maternal grandmother	*mormor* (mother's mother) (all)
maternal grandfather	*morfar* (mother's father) (all)
paternal grandmother	*farmor* (father's mother) (all)
paternal grandfather	*farfar* (father's father) (all)
great-grandmother	*oldemor* (olden mother), *gammalmormor* (S)
great-grandfather	*oldefar* (olden father), *gammalfarfar* (S)
uncle on father's side	*farbror* (father's brother) or *onkel* (N, S)
uncle on mother's side	*morbror* (mother's brother) or *onkel* (N, S)
uncle-in-law	*onkel* (D, S only)
aunt – mother's sister	*moster* (mother's sister) (S, D) or *tante* (N)
aunt – father's sister	*faster* (father's sister) (S, D) or *tante* (N)
aunt-in-law	*tante* (D, N). (*tante* in Swedish means an old lady)
cousin	*kusin* (both sexes) (S) *kusine* (female) (D, N) *fætter*/*fetter* (male) (D, N)
step-anything	add the prefix 'sted', 'ste' or 'stye' – so *stedfar* is stepfather
grandchild	*barnbarn* (S)/*barnebarn* (D, N) (child's child)
great-grandchild	*barnbarnsbarn* (S) (child's child's child)/*oldebarn* (D, N) (older's child)

Traditional Scandinavian names

Throughout history, these haven't actually changed much and, when you look across the different top ten surnames for Sweden, Denmark and Norway, they are much the same, with a few regional variations. It's one of those little things where you can see the strong connection between the Scandinavian nations.

The traditional Nordic way (except Finland) for surnames was quite simple and usually patronymic: you named your son after yourself. So, if your name was Peter, your son would be, Axel Petersson. Axel's son would then be Lars Axelsson and so on. Any daughters would have 'dotter' (for daughter) at the end – so, Hjerdis Pettersdotter. Her child would take their name from the father. This way of surnames changing with each generation vanished from Sweden, Norway and Denmark a long time ago, but is still used today in Iceland. That is why Iceland's phone book is arranged by first name, rather than surname. Looking across Norway, Sweden and Denmark, it is clear that we all come from much the same pot of patronymic surnames – these are the top ten for each country:

Denmark	Norway	Sweden
Nielsen	Hansen	Andersson
Jensen	Olsen	Eriksson
Hansen	Larsen	Gustavsson
Pedersen	Andersen	Johansson
Andersen	Pedersen	Karlsson
Christensen	Nilsen	Larsson
Larsen	Kristiansen	Nilsson
Sørensen	Jensen	Olsson
Rasmussen	Karlsen	Persson
Jørgensen	Johansen	Petersson

Other Scandinavian surnames now popular across the world also often have Nordic roots. The clues are in the ending of the name – when -sson/sen denotes that it's a son, other endings are quite often very much rooted in nature. Overleaf are usual spellings – but many variations occur in all Nordic languages in many different combinations:

5 V GULLANDER   C
    G EKLUNDH
    NETTMARK   L
    C FERNSTRÖM

4 V HANSSON
    PÅLSSON
    BERONIUS BOLIN
    STERNER

3 V EDENHÄLL
    M DROTTMAR
    SONESSON LANE
    IVARSSON G. STEIDLER G

2 V ASKERLUND
    PALM ULLERSTAM
    PINOTTI L M
    LINDQVIST FÄREGÅRD

1 V HÖRBERGER   A
    BOSTRÖM   M
    ÅKERBERG   M
    LUNDBERG   E
    ORD & SÅNT

IV   HUSBY ECKBO

III   BLOMHOFF

II   Johansen Grimsmo

I   FASTING

Andersson B & C

DeVedur A & T

Berg B & C

Ahlmann H

Björkheden–Koefoed

Berg Josefa

Nilsson

L JOHANSSON

OSKARSSON

J HENRIKSSON

Lundström

JONBORN WENTZEL

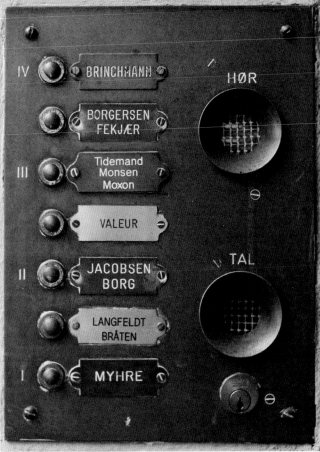

IV   BRINCHMANN

    BORGERSEN FEKJÆR

III   Tidemand Monsen Moxon

    VALEUR

II   JACOBSEN BORG

    LANGFELDT BRÅTEN

I   MYHRE

HØR

TAL

EK

MØLLE

LÖF

FALK

SKJEGGE

Ö

FISK

Ek – oak	**Eng** – meadow	**Berg** – mountain	**Ny** – new
Lund – grove	**Eld** – elder	**Lind** – lime tree	**Ö** – island
Dam – dam	**Falk** – falcon	**Ljung** – heather	**Pil** – arrow
Gaard – farm	**Fisk** – fish	**Löf** – leaf	**Sjö** – lake
Mølle – mill	**Grahn** – fir	**Høj** – mound	**Rund** – round
Strand – beach	**Bak** – hill	**Næss** – headland	**Skjegge** – beard
Sund – strait	**Hall** – hall	**Gren** – branch	**Sten** – Stone
Vang – field, meadow	**Strohm** – stream	**Qvist** – twig	
Dahl – valley	**Holm** – islet	**Skov** – woods	

The common name of Ljunggren would then be Heather-Branch. Sjölund would be Lake-Grove and so on. This list is of course not complete – many other old names can be found, but a lot of the more common non-patronymic based names contain some variation across all three countries.

In Sweden, Norway and Denmark, laws exist about what you can and can't call your child as a first name. For example, you can't name your daughter Ikea or Pluto in Denmark, you can't name your son Elvis in Sweden, nor Veranda, and you can't use a surname as a first name in Norway. On the approved lists are all the usual typically Scandinavian names. A few of these work less well abroad, but are perfectly common in Scandinavia:

Odd – Norwegian male

Love – Swedish male

Jerker – Swedish male

Bent – male name from all over Scandinavia

Even – Norwegian male

Uffe – Danish male

Fanny – Swedish female

In Norway, especially, combining first names to form a more unique name is often done. For example, Karl-Gunnar or Hans-Peter. There are twenty-two people in Norway today registered with the first name of Odd-Even.

Culture

Greetings!

Being three countries, greetings vary – here are some of the main ways:

Hej

The word *hej* or *hei* (a casual 'hello') works in Norway, Sweden and Denmark.

Hejsan is Swedish, and you'd never use it in the other countries.

Hej hej in Denmark usually means 'bye', and in Sweden, it doesn't – there you can use it as hello AND bye. It's the same in Norway.

Tjena – a common Swedish greeting.

Hej då – casual goodbye in Swedish.

Ha det – casual goodbye in Norwegian.

Tak for sidst

This literally means 'thank you for last time'. It is a very polite thing to say. Maybe you had beers with Jon yesterday and it was all *hyggeligt*, so you want to start your interaction with '*Tak for sidst*'. If you bump into Swedish Auntie Agneta, whose house you went to for crayfish supper three months ago, '*Tack för senast*' is very appropriate. You never say it to your colleagues, of course, because this is work and not that kind of together time.

Tak for sidst is polite, but it has no expiration date. *Tak for sidst* for last year's New Year's Eve party. Say it in person or on the phone.

Use it in the wrong situation and people will spot it. For example, you don't say '*Tak for sidst*' if you have a chat in a supermarket queue or had cup of coffee at the local café. However, there are no hard and fast rules. As an alternative stick with being rude and just omit using it.

How are you?

Scandinavians mainly use '*hej*' greetings, as opposed to 'How are you?' Assume that if a Scandinavian person asks you how you are, they actually want to know and will worry if they get a one-word answer.

In the same vein, if you ask a Scandinavian 'How are you?', you can expect a longer reply, mentioning the dodgy knee, a headache and whatever else might be going on in their lives.

Quick ways to annoy a Scandinavian person

Each person definitely has their own little gripes, but it's pretty certain that some things on this list will make the nostrils of most Scandinavian folk flare. Regional variations may occur.

1. **Talk about Scandinavia as if it's one country.** It's not. We're not. We are all friends but we are not one. Nobody inside Scandinavia would ever brand themselves 'Scandinavian'.
2. **Presume Scandinavia is a small place.** It's three and a half times the size of the United Kingdom. We'll show you BIG.
3. **Confuse Sweden with Switzerland.** They are not even next door to each other. Very different approaches to tax for starters.
4. **Ask if there are polar bears in Copenhagen.** Really?
5. **Sing the 'Swedish Chef Song' when you meet us.** 'Hurdy gurdy' is not how we speak. To Swedes, the Swedish Chef actually sounds more Norwegian.
6. **Don't be on time.** Seriously, what is the point of arranging a time to meet if you're going to be late. Or (god forbid) early? You have a five-minute window.
7. **Ask us why we are cold when we are used to cold weather.** Because our houses are really well insulated with good heating. We feel the cold just like you humans.
8. **Give us sinks with two taps.** How is anyone supposed to wash their hands with one burning and one ice-cold tap? This is not efficient. We like efficient.
9. **Question why we have lunch at 11.00 a.m.** Or even worse, arrange a meeting in the middle of our lunch at 11.30 a.m.
10. **Kill the cheese.** Do not make ski slopes of the cheese.
11. **Wear shoes inside in our homes.** Leave them by the door – we'll lend you a pair of slippers.
12. **Say that we don't LOOK Scandinavian.** We come in all colours and sizes.
13. **Ask us how we are – and then not wait for the answer.** But you ASKED! Now we will explain about last week's meeting at the council and Mrs Jensen's complaint about the village fête and how we woke up late. You best wait.
14. **You're Swedish? I had a Danish girlfriend once, do you know her?** See point 2.
15. **Ask why our coffee intake is the highest in the world.** We won't stop to answer. Because, well, we can't stop, need to keep moving…

Great idioms

When Scandinavians move abroad and speak another language, we often use our own idioms and translate them, literally. This does not always work well, seeing as it makes no sense in English to tell someone there are no cows on the ice. Across our countries, we really do have some great ones, many more than there's room for in this book, so here is a selection of some of the best:

Låtsas som det regnar (Swedish)
Pretend that it's raining
Meaning: Act normally, so as not to attract any attention

Født bak en brunost (Norwegian)
Born behind a brown cheese
Meaning: The person is a bit slow

Finns det hjärterum så finns det stjärterum (Swedish)
If there's room in the heart, there's room for the arse (ass)
Meaning: There's room for everyone here

Glida in på en räkmacka (Swedish)
To slide in on a prawn sandwich
Meaning: Someone didn't have to work to get where they are in life

At træde i spinaten (Danish)
To tread on the spinach
Meaning: To make a mistake, to make things worse

Även små grytor har öron (Swedish)
Even small saucepans have ears
Meaning: The kids might hear

Det blæser en halv pelican (Danish)
It's blowing half a pelican
Meaning: It's really windy

Smaken är som baken, delad (Swedish)

Taste is like your bum, divided

Meaning: There are two halves; everybody has an opinion

Hej hopp i blåbärsskogen! (Swedish)

Hello and jump in the blueberry forest!

Meaning: A cheerful expression to be used when you are a bit surprised

Nu har du skitit i det blå skåpet (Swedish)

Now you have shit in the blue cupboard

Meaning: When you really have made a fool of yourself

Bæsje på leggen (Norwegian)

To poo on your calf

Meaning: To make a mistake

Å svelge noen kameler (Norwegian)

To swallow camels

Meaning: To give in, admit defeat

Å være midt i smørøyet (Norwegian)
To be in the middle of the butter melting in the porridge
Meaning: To be in a very favourable place or situation

At hoppe på limpinden (Danish)
To jump on the glue stick
Meaning: To take the bait

Ingen fara på taket (Swedish)
No danger on the roof
Meaning: No worries

Han tog benene på nakken (Danish)
He took his legs on the back of his neck
Meaning: He hurried up

Det är ingen ko på isen (Swedish)
There are no cows on the ice
Meaning: Nothing to worry about

Du er helt ude og cykle (Danish)
You're completely out cycling
Meaning: You're completely wrong

Er det hestens fødselsdag? (Danish)
Is it the horse's birthday?
Meaning: The rye bread is cut too thick on my open sandwich

Jeg aner ugler i mosen (Danish)
I suspect owls in the bog
Meaning: Something fishy going on

At være oppe på lakridserne (Danish)
To be up on the liquorice
Meaning: To be on it, full of energy

Når lykken kommer rekende på en fjøl (Norway)
When happiness is served to you on a chopping board
Meaning: To have things handed to you on a plate in life

The Law of Jante

Across all of Scandinavia, a peculiar set of laws exists. Not mentioned, but always there, silently enforced by everybody in unison. This is the Laws of Jante.

In 1933, a novel called *A Fugitive Crosses His Tracks* was published by Norwegian–Danish writer Aksel Sandemose. This novel describes the author's alter ego, Espen, a sailor who sets about discovering himself through his childhood in a town that Sandemose refers to as 'Jante'. A huge sensation when it was first published, this novel is raw and bitter and takes shape through the unwritten laws of the town of Jante:

The Ten Rules of Jante

1. Don't think *you* are anything special.
2. Don't think *you* are as good as *we* are.
3. Don't think *you* are smarter than *we* are.
4. Don't convince yourself that *you* are better than *we* are.
5. Don't think *you* know more than *we* do.
6. Don't think *you* are more important than *we* are.
7. Don't think *you* are good at anything.
8. Don't laugh at *us*.
9. Don't think anyone cares about *you*.
10. Don't think *you* can teach *us* anything.

Janteloven (the Law of Jante) isn't unlike most countries' cultural codes to ensure some sort of peace is upheld. However, because the laws are actually formalised by Sandemose, these cultural values became much starker and obvious when seen in print.

To understand how they are applied so strongly in Scandinavia, you need to look at our general culture: Scandinavians love being equal. We like having the same car as the neighbour, we like earning similar salaries. We like not having a huge class divide. It means we are all sort of on a level playing field and it makes us content. It is how we preserve harmony and social stability, to an extent. It has existed for many years, even before it was written down – and can be found in old sayings such as the Swedish proverb: 'Noble deeds are done in silence'.

Many people think the Law of Jante is something consciously applied. We do not, however, have Jante-enforcement officers hanging around street corners, trying to catch people out who are getting too big for their boots. The reality is much more subtle: it stirs.

In addition, the Law of Jante is not so much about people not wanting to see you drive down the high street in your new Volvo XC90 – it is much more about making sure Bjørn Pedersen down the road doesn't feel bad that he doesn't have one. The first would be simple envy, but it goes deeper than that. Indeed, when you look at how the Law of Jante is applied across cultural norms in Scandinavia, it is perhaps also easier to see how many democratic social policies have been easily accepted. It is not because of you, it is because of others around you. The greater good, all of us and our collective social happiness.

Things are changing, however, as the world gets smaller and our cultural norms are shifting slightly with the influence of the more capitalist mindset of the have-it-all and the look-at-me-how-great-I-am culture. We're all a bit more bling and we are brave enough to stand out more. People who have built successful businesses are ok to talk about it now and, by and large, being successful is ok (as long as you don't claim all the praise for yourself). As long as you share your new-found status and wealth with society, you are fine to have it. There are, however, some areas that are culturally unacceptable to cross:

- You do not ask a Scandinavian what they earn.
- You do not brag about yourself, ever.
- No need to buy rounds in bars; you will be bankrupt – *and* will stand out, because Scandinavians don't like to be indebted, so will simply insist on repaying everything to be equal.

Indeed, you can easily still spot *Janteloven* still in use in everyday conversation with Scandinavians from any of the countries. If a Scandinavian person is singled out for doing

a really good job, they will immediately say it was only possible because of their team and dismiss personal efforts. Thinking of running for class rep? Wait for someone to nominate you. Just hit a number one in the charts with your new song? You only got there because people bought the record. It is never about you, it is always about us.

You are free to do anything you want and can in Scandinavia – as long as you don't appear different to any of us and stand out. Ever. And perhaps forget about that new shiny Volvo for now until you understand the social rules.

How to lagom

Lagom is the most important Swedish word you will ever learn. It goes deep into the make-up of every Swede, at home or abroad, and is part of being quintessentially Swedish. The word *lagom* is said to derive from the folk etymology in a phrase used in Viking times: *laget om* – meaning 'around to the team' – which was allegedly used to describe just how much mead one should drink when passing the horn around in the group. This etymology is commonly accepted to be right, although some parallels are made with the Law of Jante and the common set of rules about how much one should have of something – again, things go back to the greater good for the whole group.

The word means 'just right'. It also means 'just enough', 'sufficient', 'the correct amount'. In Finnish, the word is *sopiva*; in Norwegian and Danish, the word *tilpasselig* is the most fitting. It means 'not too much, not too little' and also means 'fair share'. This single word denotes all of those meanings, simply depending on the context in which you use it.

There is an old saying in Sweden, *lagom är bäst* ('*lagom* is best'), which really sums up how Swedes think and act in everyday life:

How big a slice of cake would you like? *Lagom.*

How are you? *Lagom.*

The weather is *lagom.*

You drink a *lagom* amount of wine.

To understand *lagom*, you first need to first understand the Scandinavians – in particular, Swedish cultural psyche, which is one of consensus and equality for all. Swedes don't overdo anything, there are no over-the-top buildings, no flashy show-offs. Everything is middle of the road, fair and just the right amount.

People often wonder why, with the amount of cake we eat in Scandinavia and the number of sweets consumed, are we not all as big as houses. It's because, well, *lagom*. Most Scandinavians won't have two buns with their *fika* break, only one. One of those big bags of to-share crisps may be opened alone, but you won't eat it all in one sitting. There will be mayonnaise on the open sandwiches, but it's on one slice of rye bread, making it all very *lagom* and balanced. 'Super-size' in fast-food restaurants isn't really that popular – it just isn't *lagom*.

It's impossible to define the word *lagom* as a specific amount because it varies so much between people. How much cake is it appropriate to eat? How hot is *lagom* when it comes to your coffee? It's a feeling, it's something engrained in the culture and psyche of the people that is almost impossible to learn. But the amazing thing is: if a Swede asks you how much coffee you want and you say *lagom*, they will know *exactly* what you mean.

Hygge (who-guh)

The word *hygge* can be traced back to the nineteenth century and stems from the Germanic and Old Norse word *hyggja* that meant to feel satisfied, to mean and to think. The word exists in most of the Nordic languages (*mys* in Swedish and *kos* in Norwegian) although it is now mainly used day-to-day in Danish. In fact, the Danes have built their whole cultural identity around *hygge* – it is part of what makes Denmark Danish and what makes the Danish person who he or she is. It is in every aspect of Danish life, from how they spend their weekend evenings to how they cope with long winters. It's in how they eat, how they socialise and how they create their living spaces.

The first thing to be aware of when defining *hygge* is that it is not the same as 'cosy'. The difference is that cosy is a physical definition – the armchair can be cosy, the house can be cosy – but this does not mean that people in the chair are having a *hyggelig* time or that the house is *hyggeligt*. This is because *hygge* is not a physical description, but rather a state of mind. The special thing is that this state of mind takes place in a space that is shared with others and where some physical elements help emphasise those feelings. Think of the word 'hug', which also stems back to the word *hyggja*. A hug is similar in that it can only be a good hug if you create a connection with the person. A hug – like *hygge* – has warmth, comfort, time and love.

In recent years, people across the globe have woken up to the idea of *hygge*. Books have been written on the concept, shops have opened that promise to make your search for ultimate *hygge* easier (usually selling scented candles). It doesn't quite work like that; that is the equivalent of buying a new pair of yoga pants to make yourself into an instant yogi. Because *hygge* is not something you search for – you already have it, you're already doing it. People have started to describe *hygge* as some sort of mindfulness, a new 'it' thing that will help change your life and teach you how to be a better person. You won't find any Scandinavians overcomplicating the feeling like that. *Hygge* isn't mindfulness, *hygge* is just you, in a chilled-out state, with nice people and a bar of chocolate or a glass of wine.

Do you remember that time when you were sitting in a welcoming space, surrounded by people you love, and someone lit a few candles and put a bowl of snacks on the table? That was *hygge*. It was *hygge* because you made time to feel it. This is also the feeling that made the whole thing memorable and it's why you remember it now, so fondly. It's as simple as that.

People also seem very busy trying to define *hygge* as something that can only take place on dark evenings. This is not true – *hygge* can take place at any time of the year, any hour of the day. It's just easier to feel it when we are not busy running from place to place

during the day. It's easier to find the time when we are in a place of comfort and, let's face it, this does not usually happen on bus 18 on the way to work. But it could, if we ever let it.

Hygge can also be combined with seasons and events. Add the word 'Christmas' in front of hygge (Julehygge), and you instantly get the feeling of cosy living rooms, decorated real trees, giving presents, eating ginger biscuits. Danish food magazines are full of Julehygge special issues all through December. Equally, Sommerhygge means you and the people you love, sitting in the garden, the kids running around; maybe you are reading a book and eating a piece of cake. Feriehygge is holiday hygge. There is Easter hygge, too. Then there is Fredaghygge, which takes place on Friday evenings with family and friends, or just weekend hygge, which is the whole weekend when you have no plans at all apart from just being and doing what you feel like. And there is definitely not a scented candle that can span through all of those – it has to come from within. It starts inside you.

Five things that will help you create a feeling of *hygge*

Time. You have to make time for it – it can't have a planned end. You can't set aside an hour to *hygge*, because then it will not be an undefined time period.

Nice people. While you can absolutely *hygge* with yourself, it is much easier to do it with other people around. It's impossible to *hygge* with people you don't like or know – there has to be a personal connection.

Food. The addition of a bowl of crisps or sweets does not in itself create *hygge*, but it speeds up the feeling of *hygge* immensely. It won't usually work with a bowl of salad.

Candles and little lamps. Turn off the big lights, light candles, switch on the lamps and feel the *hygge* come alive. *Hygge* is also greatly increased by the addition of a log fire.

Woolly socks. While wearing woollies alone won't put you in the *hygge* mood, if you combine it with all of the above, it is likely you will have created a space in time where woolly socks can help you feel more comfortable. Alternatively, wear something snug and comfortable to help you relax, like one of those massive blankets with built-in slippers.

The items of clothing themselves have little to do with *hygge*, but when you are wearing them, you are unlikely to rush out and do other stuff. It signals you are already winding down. That said, if you are inviting Scandi friends over for a *hyggelig* dinner, and you open the door wearing a blanket all-in-one, they are likely to think you are completely mad. Everything in proportion here – the most important thing is just to chill out and stop forcing it to happen.

Top ten Vikings

As the Vikings travelled, traded and raided across the world, some deserve a special mention. Granted, none are famous for charitable causes and possibly they are infamous rather than famous, but the Vikings played a huge role in our world for several hundred years, which is still evident in places today.

The Viking period is documented through the sagas of the time (often written much later) and other historical documents. A lot of what we know has come from legends and folktales, so the exact details are often blurred. Many of the tales are still thrilling to read, but we're thankful Scandinavia is a much calmer place now. Here are some favourites:

Eysteinn Fart
736–780, Eysteinn Hálfdansson

His real name was Eysteinn Hálfdansson, but in one of the sagas he is named as Eysteinn Fart. Even today, 'fart' means 'speed' in Scandinavia, so it could have been a compliment to his sailing skills. He died suddenly when he was blown off his ship by a gust of wind.

Ragnar Hairy Breeches
9th Century, Ragnarr Loðbrók

It is hard to pin down who Ragnar was. His life is written about across different lands and times and it is quite possible that this character was actually a king or ruler under a different name – half-legend, half-reality (or he lived over a hundred years and was capable of being in two places at once). In fact, he might never have existed at all – but for the sake of this entry, let's assume he did and so the legend of Ragnar Hairy Breeches (he is rumoured to have worn trousers of animal skins made for him by his wife) lives on.

Ragnar apparently married three times. His most notable was the awesome and fearless Lagertha (more about her later). He also fathered many, many sons in many places – most notably Sigurd Snake-in-the-Eye and Ivar the Boneless.

While historians disagree about almost everything concerning Ragnar, his saga probably ended after he was captured by Anglo-Saxon King Ælla of Northumbria, who threw him into a pit of snakes. Legend has it some of his sons vowed to avenge their father's death and crossed the North Sea in 866 seeking revenge. Some say they succeeded after a particularly gruesome torture, while others say Ælla survived only to die in another battle at York the following year.

RAGNARR LOÐBRÓK

HLAÐGERÐR

HARALÐR BLÁTONN GORMSSON

OGMUND

Harald Bluetooth
935–985, Haraldr blátonn Gormsson

Here was a Viking who was really good at getting different camps to collaborate and link up and he is famous for unifying Norway and Denmark.

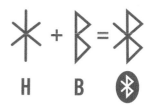

It is from Harald that today's Bluetooth technology takes its name, connecting everything in your home wirelessly. That little icon you see when the Bluetooth is connected is actually rune letters, spelling out Harald Bluetooth's initials.

Erik the Red
950–1003, Eiríkr hinn rauði

Real name Erik Þorvaldsson, this ginger beast of a Viking is mostly famous for founding the first Norse settlement in Greenland. Erik, a Norwegian settler on Iceland, was banished following the death of a few locals. A master of marketing, he deliberately named his new home 'Greenland' to be more appealing to other potential settlers (having witnessed Iceland's misstep in not naming their island 'valleys of green and deliciously warm earth showers'). Once he got people to Greenland, well, it was too late.

Leif Eriksson
970–1020, Leifr Eiríksson

Son of Erik the Red and brother of Freydís, Leif continued his father's journey westwards and is recognised as being the first European to set foot in North America, landing in 'Vínland' (modern-day Newfoundland), as he is thought to have called it, some 500 years before Christopher Columbus.

Freydís Eríksdóttir
970–unknown

Leif's sister Freydís was a formidable Viking warrior in her own right. In the Saga of Erik the Red, Freydís traded with Native Americans until a large bull went berserk. Amid the confusion, battle ensued and as a group surrounded Freydís (who was pregnant at the time) she ripped open her clothes to bare her breast and the sword she was carrying next to it. The men ran away in fear. In the Saga of the Greenlanders though, Freydís was less celebrated after she lied to her husband, accusing two brothers of beating her. The brothers and their men were killed for their supposed crime, but Freydís killed their women too after her husband refused to do so, and lied to her brother Leif about what happened. Later on, Freydís' descendants were all virtually ostracised from society because of her actions.

King Cnut the Great
995–1035, Knútr inn ríki

Cnut was the Danish king who continues to give proofreaders a headache, which is probably why he is also known more safely as Canute. He was also king of Norway and England, as ruler of the so-called North Sea Empire. Cnut gets a raw deal from history following the story called 'King Canute and the Waves' (not to be confused with the band that won Eurovision in 1997). It tells of how Cnut demonstrated to his court that he had no power over the sea, because he wasn't God. Which is very wise. However, somewhere along the line, someone decided to reverse the story so that Cnut was deluded enough to believe he could control the waves. An early incidence of fake news.

Harald Hardrada
1015–1066, Haraldr Sigurðarson

1066 was a big year for England – and Harald III, King of Norway, was one of its first casualties. He spent most of his young life in battles, starting at home before fighting his way through eastern Europe all the way to Constantinople, where he became the leader of the Varangian Guard, part of the Byzantine Army. After returning home to claim the throne, Harald spent a lot of time raiding Denmark and trying to become its king, before setting his sights on England. Big mistake. After a successful fight near York, Harald was killed at the ferocious Battle of Stamford Bridge by the forces of King Harold II, and many historians say Harald's death marked the end of the Viking age. However, there was a nasty twist in the saga for the victor. After Harold defeated Harald, William the Conqueror's forces arrived from France just a couple of days later, and the English king was killed the following month at the Battle of Hastings.

Ogmund Tangle-Hair

With a fleeting appearance in Njál's Saga, Ogmund Tangle-Hair is more of a one-line character than a major star (and gets killed in his scene, too). He is included only for having the best Viking name (it was either him or Ulf the Unwashed).

Lagertha
9th Century, Hlaðgerðr

Like her one-time husband Ragnar, we're not really clear who Lagertha was, or precisely what happened to her – some have speculated that her story has been influenced by other tales of female deities mentioned in the sagas. Lagertha was a hugely impressive woman (by Viking standards – I don't advocate most of the things she got up to). She chose to become a shieldmaiden – a female warrior – and apparently her male counterparts were all staggered to see her excellent fighting skills while wearing her hair down. After marrying Lagertha, fickle Ragnar dumped her for a Swedish princess. However, when he got into trouble during a later battle, Lagertha still came to his aid, bringing 120 ships for him. Gathering that many ships in Viking times was no small accomplishment, so her loyalty is all the more impressive.

Nordic mythical creatures

We all think it's quite cute that over half of Icelandic people believe in elves. Roads are planned and re-routed according to spots where elves are said to be living. House plans are re-done if they cross an elf path. Still, the underlying roots of our history and culture also have a lot of little – and big – creatures. Even if we don't always admit to still believing in them, they do creep into the everyday Scandinavian culture, especially on high days and holidays.

Nisser/tomter

Usually no taller than a few feet, a *tomte* (Swedish) or *nisse* (Danish, Norwegian) is most prevalent at Christmas time, but is present all year round in every household. Usually depicted as male (although both *nisse*-mammas and *nisse*-children exist, too), he generally has a white beard and wears a red or grey woolly hat. They can be nice or naughty, usually depending on how you treat them.

The word originates from the creatures taking care of the farm or stables – and a house plot was known as a *tomt*, which is where the Swedish name comes from. In places, his name was often Nils and a common nickname for someone called Nils is *Nisse*, which is how he is known by different names.

In Sweden, it is the *tomte*, not Santa, who brings presents for the children. In Denmark, you have to put out a bowl of rice porridge for your house *nisse* on Christmas Eve. If you do not, you will anger him and for the rest of the year he will play tricks on you. Hiding the remote control, stealing your socks, scaring the cat – and anything you can't explain by normal means – will be the fault of the *nisse*.

nisse

Huldra

Deep in the forest, the *huldra* lives. A *huldra* is a stunning, seductive female creature – you'll know her by the crown of flowers in her hair. She is fair in looks and her voice is beautiful. From the front she looks human, but from the back you will see she has a cow's tail (in Sweden, it's a fox's tail). Her back looks like a hollowed-out tree. The word *huldra* means 'hidden'.

The *huldra* was known to seduce young men, taking them with her to the mountains, where she begged them to marry her. Legend has it that if a man does marry her, she will turn ugly, but her strength will be that of ten men and she'll lose her tail.

The *huldra* will treat you as you treat her. Be nice and she is nice back and showers you with gifts. Be mean and betray her and she will punish you worse than you can imagine. She also knows all the best fishing spots. Surely a bonus if you are considering marrying one.

The *huldra* is also known as *skogsrå* (forest spirit) or *Tallemaja* (pine tree Mary) in Sweden and it is also the name of an oil field in the North Sea, which has little to do with forest creatures. In Norway, there is a male form of the *huldra*, known as the *huldrekall*.

Tusser

A Norwegian *tusse* (or just *tuss*) lives underground, often near humans. The name has its roots from 'troll', but *tusser* are smaller, more goblin-like, and intelligent too. It's often said the male version of a *huldra* looks like a *tusse* – ugly little things with big noses. Their job is to take care of the livestock, mainly. Before entering a stable in Norway, you must warn the *tusse* you are coming. If you do not, you may startle and anger him. Also, be careful when walking around because if you step on his roof (usually soft moss), he gets really annoyed. And it is not hard to annoy him.

Nøkkar

Nøkk is a water spirit. He is evil and he is a shape-shifter. He lives in the water under the water lilies and will drag down anyone who dares to pick them. His skin is like that of a corpse, his eyes are yellow and his teeth razor-sharp. He will shape-shift to anything he pleases so as to get to you more easily and is specially

TUSSE

active on Midsummer's Eve, Christmas and on Thursdays. To protect yourself from him, say 'Nøkken Nøkken' and throw a steel cross in the water. Related to the Scottish kelpie, a *nøkk* is also known as *näkk* in Sweden and in English as a nixie or a neck. In Scandinavia, *nøkkar* are male while in Germany, they were usually female and were the River Rhine mermaids. The word *nøkk* comes from the Old Norse *nykr*, meaning 'river horse'.

Elves and dwarves

In Norse mythology, the elf and dwarf live in opposite worlds: one is light and one is dark. The elves are more beautiful than the sun itself. They have the power to bring illness, but also to heal. There are tales of elf–human relationships, producing elf-like children, too. These children look human, but also elfin and have magical powers. Elves are closely linked to small fairies and may be one and the same. They love dancing in the morning dew. If you ever see mist on a lake or field in the early morning, it is sure to be an *älvdans* ('elf dance'). Do not disturb them, because they do not appreciate this and may lure you in, and everyone knows that elves can dance a man to death.

On the flipside to the elves sit the dwarves. They are small, definitely not as beautiful as the sun, human-like creatures, who usually live in the mountains. These wise men do mining and crafting and are very hardworking. Mythical dwarves don't have much contact with humans and are not considered scary. They can be invisible, at will. The Poetic Edda contains hundreds of references to the dwarves, but in the Icelandic Poetic Edda collection of works they are referenced as only four: North, East, South and West – the four dwarves who hold up the sky.

Trolls

Big, dumb, evil trolls. The verb 'to troll' stems from *trylle*, meaning to bewitch and conjure. Trolls may be another version of the *jötunn* from Norse mythology. They are big, ogre-like creatures, who live under bridges, in caves and in the mountains. Trolls are not helpful to humans and they are not very bright, either. They are considered dangerous, so you should not approach or interact with them if you meet one. They tend to turn to stone when exposed to sunlight, so they roam at night. If you see an unusually large boulder in the middle of a field, this is probably a troll who went out during the day. Trolls live with other trolls in small family units.

Trolls are frightened by lightning and because trolls never converted to Christianity, they also hate church bells, so if you stay inside the towns, you are usually fine. If you see one, be aware he may have up to twelve heads and only one eye. Don't be alarmed, this is perfectly normal. You can usually outwit a troll easily, so just make sure any reaction you have is a smart one.

Fossegrim

Neither good nor bad male spirit who lives in a waterfall and spends his days and nights playing the fiddle. He never tires of it. He can be persuaded to help aspiring fiddle players, too – bring a lump of meat or other goodies, and *Fossegrim* will teach you how to play. *Fossegrim* never leaves his waterfall, so lessons at your house are out – you have to go to him.

Pesta

In Nordic folklore, *Pesta* is an old woman dressed in black. Sometimes, she carries a rake, sometimes a broom. If she turns up at your farm with a broom, only some people on the farm will die. A rake, and you're all toast. 'The Pest' was another term for the Bubonic plague. Stories of this old witch-like creature travelling from farm to farm began to emerge in the fourteenth century.

The basics of Scandinavian politics

It's fair to say that, when looking at Scandinavian political parties, applying 'left' and 'right' to them doesn't make it clear. Left in Scandinavia is so far left and the right is not so right. By and large, we hang quite left of left, even when we're right.

It is also tricky to sum up three different countries and their political standpoints in a few hundred words without delivering only the key points. It is far too complex and politics is constantly moving: opinions change, governments get thrown out, and things start over. Also, there is no room to talk about *Borgen* and how the eponymous Birgitte Nyborg should be in charge of everything.

Suffice to say, certain things ring true across the countries, which also goes to show how similar our values are that, on the whole, tie us together as Scandinavia while remaining separate countries, too. In general, governments in Scandinavia are considered to be for the people, by the people. There is a trust in government and the system not often as strong in other Western countries. The 'we're all in this together' approach means high turn outs at elections and political engagement across the board.

Norway: More than 78 per cent of Norwegians headed out to vote in the last general election. These elections are usually held every four years. The government in Norway is generally believed to be working for and on behalf of the people. It is a large social democracy, made up of a lot of small parties that have to work together in a coalition in order to form any sort of majority government. Because of the large number of small parties, politics usually has to be carried out fairly and efficiently with little mudslinging, as most will have to find a way to work together at some point or another. At the time of writing, the current prime minister is the Conservative Erna Solberg.

Sweden: There are eight officially registered parties in Sweden (the biggest being the Social Democrats, the Moderates and the Centre Party). They also have a whole load of smaller ones – including many joke parties: Donald Duck Party, Booze Party. General elections are held every four years. The last election had over 85 per cent voter turn out. In recent years, there has been a steep rise in the popularity of more right-wing parties. The current government is a minority coalition between the Social Democrats and the Greens, with Social Democrat Stefan Löfven as the prime minister as I write.

Denmark: No single party has held absolute majority in government since the beginning of the twentieth century. Nine parties are currently represented in government and any party with more than two per cent of the vote is assured parliamentary representation. Government is always a form of coalition and usually runs with a minority, too.

The main parties were always the Conservatives, the Social Democrats, the Left Party – *Venstre*, although, confusingly, *Venstre* (literally meaning 'left') is actually quite right of

centre and not that left at all – and the Danish Social Liberal Party. With the sharp rise in right-wing anti-immigration party support, the Danish People's Party won huge backing during the general election of 2015. Elections are also held every four years and turn out at the most recent was 85.8 per cent. The current government (at the time of writing) is a single-party minority government, led by *Venstre*'s Lars Løkke Rasmussen as prime minister.

The most basic of basic Norse mythology

Scandinavians are a little conflicted at times. Christianity is the main religion, but pagan roots shine through in our heritage and there is always that little bit of Odin and Thor running through our veins. Perhaps the mythology and belief in the old ways are left over from all those years before the Vikings became Christians. Many of our celebrations are still connected to the cycle of the year, the pagan traditions and beliefs. To get a brief overview of what is a very large collection of sagas, we need to start from the beginning:

Yggdrasil

In Norse mythology, the earth is a flat disc and that disc is the branches of the cosmological tree of life, Yggdrasil. This tree, supposedly an Ash, links the nine worlds (Asgard, Vanaheimr, Álfheimr, Niðavellir, Jötunheimr, Niflheim, Muspelheim, Midgard and Hel) together. The tree has three axes and therefore three levels of worlds. In the centre of this world is Asgard, land of Æsir, which is where the gods lived. You can only get to Asgard if you cross a bridge called Bifröst – actually, it is a flaming rainbow, not really a bridge. Bifröst connects Asgard and Midgard. You then have the frost giants – they live in a place called Jötunheimr, which means 'the Giant Place'. In the south, the fire giants rule in a place called Muspelheim. In the north, a dark place called Niflheim was ruled by Hel, daughter of Loki the trickster god. Dead people usually end up here. Midgard is the place for the living man and lies between Asgard and Niflheim. Álfheimr is the home of the light elves, lighter than even the sun. Vanaheimr is home to the wise, to fertility and future-tellers – the home of Vanir. Niðavellir is the land of dwarves, or possibly of dark elves, and called Svartálfheirur, it's all a bit complicated. Hel, which shares the same name as the goddess, is possibly the origin of the English word 'hell'. Visitors had a varied reception.

Valhalla

The hall in Asgard presided over by Odin where those who died in battle await Ragnarök. If you die in battle, half of you go to Valhalla, which is better than going to Niflheimr, which is where most go when they die a normal death. The Valkyries choose who gets slain in battle.

Ragnarök

Ragnarök refers to a great battle that ultimately results in the death of major gods, including Odin, Thor, Freya and Loki. It also tells the story of natural disasters and the world being

submerged in water. When all this has ended, the world is reborn again, fresh and new and fertile – and the surviving gods will meet and the world will be re-populated by two human survivors. A few years ago, Ragnarök was supposedly near, but seeing as we're still here, perhaps there was a calculation error.

How things began

First, there was fire and ice and two worlds, Muspelheim and Niflheim. When the hot air from one hit the cold air from the other, the giant (*jötunn*) Ymir and the icy cow Auðumbla were created. Then Ymir's armpit made a woman and his foot made a man. From his sweat he made the fire giant Surtr. The cow then licked a stone and a man called Búri grew out from it. Búri fathered a son called Bar and this was the father of the three gods: Odin, Vili and Ve.

The gods then killed Ymir and created another seven worlds. They used his blood to make oceans and his brain for clouds. His bones were useful as stones and heaven was made from his skull.

The three little gods went out walking one day and saw two tree stumps. They decided to make these into Embla – the first woman – and Ask – the first man. Odin made them come to life, Ve made them able to speak, see and hear, and Vili gave them their minds. The gods created Middle Earth for them and then fenced it all the way along with Ymir's eyelashes to keep out the other giants.

The gods

The Norse gods are depicted in the sagas from the ninth century. All the stories of them were passed down through poetry via the Edda and other texts in the centuries that followed and have shaped our understanding of the gods.

There are many, many gods – some are similar and likely the same, some stand out and are well known in popular culture today. Among the top gods are:

Baldr – Son of Odin and Frigg. A kind, gentle god, who is due to return after Ragnarök. Associated with light, peace, love and happiness.

Loki – The anti-hero, trickster, shape-shifter. Son of giants, but became a god anyway. God of mischief. Father of Hel. Caused the death of Baldr and is now trapped until Ragnarök comes around.

Freya – Goddess of love, of sex and fertility, war, death and gold. Her name means 'lady'. Has a cart pulled by two cats. Sister of Freyr.

Freyr – One of the most important gods in Norse mythology. Freyr means 'lord' and he was god of peace and fertility and had close links to the sun. He was 'hated by none' and always swanned around with a massive erection. You can do that when you are god of fertility, you see, nobody minds. Seen as an ancestor to the Swedish royal house.

Frigg – The highest-ranking goddess and a *völva* (shaman). Wife of Odin and mother of Baldr.

Heimdallr – The watchman of the gods and guarder of Bifröst, the rainbow bridge to Asgard. Loves all things gold. Son of nine mothers.

Hel – Goddess, ruler of Helheim, the realm of the dead in Niflheim. Daughter of Loki.

Iðun – The goddess of spring and rejuvenation and keeper of the magic apples of immortality. Had some run-ins with Loki.

Odin – The undisputed king of the Norse gods. He was the god of battle, poetry and death and he was also the Chief of Æsir. He had one eye. Married to Frigg. Father of Baldr.

Thor – The god of thunder, of the sky and of fertility. Likely the guardian of the Norse gods, he ensured order in Asgard. He was the son of Odin. When it thunders, it is Thor who rides his chariot pulled by goats in the sky – and throws his hammer, Mjölnir.

Týr – One of the principle gods of war, along with Thor and Odin. Unfortunately Fenrir the wolf bit off his hand.

Sága – Odin's drinking companion and all-round goddess.

Ullr – God of skiing. And archery, but mainly skiing. He was *really* good at it. You have to be good at stuff to be the god of it. Slalom and everything.

Kings and queens

For such equal-rights-for-all minded countries, the Scandinavians still absolutely adore their royal families. Perhaps this is partially because the Scandinavian royals are not as royal as in other countries, or, at least, they don't act as if they are. Mostly, they are seen as representatives, but do not set themselves particularly highly above everybody else. Calls to abolish the monarchies are very rare in Scandinavia.

In Norway, the king is not known as the King of Norway but, rather wonderfully, Norway's King. King Harald V is married to Queen Sonja and they have two children. Crown Prince Haakon married for true love. Crown Princess Mette-Marit was a divorced single mother with a son, Marius. The couple have two children together, Princess Ingrid and Prince Sverre. Daughter Princess Märtha is a tax payer by choice and is a trained physiotherapist, but works in alternative holistic medicine. She also claims she can communicate with angels. On top of this, she has written children's books and is an accomplished singer, appearing in choirs. Princess Märtha was married to author Ari Behn and they have three daughters, Maud, Leah and Emma.

Denmark's queen is called Margrethe, but is often referred to as Daisy, as it is her favourite flower. She is married to Henrik, Prince of Denmark, who is originally from France, where he still has a vineyard. Now retired, over the years Prince Henrik has many times voiced his unhappiness about not becoming king – merely Prince Consort, a title he renounced in 2016. Queen Margrethe is an extremely talented linguist as well as an artist, in many media from paintings to fashion design and illustrations. She is a chain smoker, often seen puffing away, and has never made any apologies for her continued cigarette smoking. The couple have two sons.

Crown Prince Frederik married a woman called Mary from Tasmania, who is now mother to his four children and is a Crown Princess. Mary is extremely popular in Denmark – and Australia. The second son, Prince Joachim, has two children with his first wife, Alexandra, and two children with his second wife, Princess Marie, who is French.

In Sweden, King Carl XVI Gustaf is married to Queen Silvia. Together they have three children. Crown Princess Victoria married her gym instructor, Daniel, who is now a prince and father of their two children, Princess Estelle and Prince Oscar. Prince Carl Philip, a very handsome prince (likely the owner of a white horse or two), married ex-glamour model Sofia. They have one son, Prince Alexander. Princess Madeleine, the youngest, married British–American financier Christopher O'Neill and the couple have two children, Princess Leonore and Prince Nicolas.

How to drink like a Scandinavian

The Nordic people, in general, have a bit of a reputation for being fond of the odd tipple. Right back to the Viking times, we have made a name for ourselves by not turning down a drink and a singsong. Being very reserved people to begin with, a drink loosens us up and makes us chat to people around us. Medicinally, a bit of a drink helps on those dark winter days, too.

In Sweden and Norway, however, you can't just pop down to the shop to buy some beer or wine. Alcohol that is over a certain percentage is still only sold at state-governed stores. In Sweden, all alcohol over 3.5 per cent (4.7 per cent in Norway) can only be sold in these state stores. In Sweden, such stores are called Systembolaget ('System Company'). In Norway, the name is Vinmonopolet ('Wine Monopoly'), which sounds like a really fun game, but is actually a shop. They are not designed with the purpose of enjoying shopping in mind, but purely functional. There is no encouragement to buy more than you planned.

All the government stores have strict opening times, so you need to plan ~~getting drunk~~ drinking sensible amounts in advance. The age limit to buy in these stores is twenty years old and you will absolutely be asked to show your ID. The government booze shops usually close before other retail stores – and always early on Saturdays. They are never, ever open on Sundays. If you've forgotten that neighbours are popping over, you'll be completely stuck – aside from a few bottles of 3.5 per cent alcohol from the local supermarket. In this case, you will have to offer them the last drops of that Cuban rum you brought back from your trip in 1993. In Norway, Vinmonopolet is also always closed on voting days, to prevent people casting their votes in an intoxicated state. So, if you ever fancy some good, old-fashioned drunken-voting and you happen to be eligible to vote in Norway, make sure you plan in advance.

The history of government-run alcohol shops goes back to Prohibition times in the early 1900s. Scandinavians used to overindulge quite a bit and were rather fond of making their own moonshine. Nowadays, rules are still in place to regulate consumption – and to ensure the state gets *all* the profits. Alcohol across the Nordic countries is not cheap by any standards – from shops to bars, you will be paying heavily for your booze to ensure you don't overdo it and that, if you do, the state benefits. It is worth noting that, in Sweden especially, the same duty applies to all wine, regardless of quality – so, if you are in the market for really good vintage wine, Sweden works out well priced for the quality – and they employ the very best wine buyers in the whole region too.

Across all the Nordic countries, you will find most homes will consume boxed wines. There is no stigma attached to them. There are several reasons for this, with Scandi efficiency brains in gear: the wine doesn't go off, which means it will last even if you don't drink for a while. The quality will usually be good, again because of the expert wine buyers. It's cost-effective, as there is less glass involved. Nobody can tell that you had two glasses while you were cooking your meatballs. They also fit nicely into refrigerators. Around 57 per cent of wine sales in Sweden are boxed wines.

Denmark, however, does not have such restrictions. While alcohol is still relatively expensive compared to other EU countries, it is cheaper than in Sweden and (most expensive) Norway. Therefore, Scandinavians go on Booze Safaris. One of the biggest Swedish 'System Company' shops is in Strömstad, close to the Norwegian border. However, day trippers from Norway can't officially bring much alcohol back home so they either smuggle it in or drink it all before going back. Stray Norwegians can sometimes be found wandering around outer Strömstad with a glazed look on their faces.

Consuming booze in bars in Denmark, Sweden and Norway requires a hefty bank balance. Your best option is local beer and the house wine is often reasonably priced. Once you head into cocktails and spirits, you have to consider choosing between being able to pay next month's rent or buying that lovely Swedish blonde next to you a piña colada. For this reason, buying rounds in Scandinavia is usually only done between very good friends.

Best Scandinavian words with no equivalent

Arbejdsglæde (Sweden, Norway, Denmark)
Literally, 'work happiness'. The joy you feel when you like your job.

Attpåklatt (Norway)
Literally meaning 'a dollop on top', this is a child born a long time after the main flock of children. In Danish, it is *efternøler* ('late runner').

Badkruka (Sweden)
Someone who refuses to get in the water. As in 'Get in the lake, you *badkruka*.'

Dygn, Døgn (Sweden, Norway, Denmark)
A period of twenty-four hours. *Døgn*, rather than 'day', is used often, in sentences like 'He was away for three *dygn*.'

Dryg (Sweden)
One word, three meanings and no translation. It can mean having a little bit more, or if it's about a person, it means someone who is a bit obnoxious. It can also refer to something lasting longer.

Dyktig (Sweden, Norway, Denmark)
A word often said to children, it means 'to be quite good at something'. It's often used as an encouragement.

Folkefest (Norway)
Literally, 'people party'. Any large gathering of happy people – a town fête, etc. – is a *folkefest*.

Forgårs (Sweden, Norway, Denmark)
The day before yesterday – literally, 'before-yesterday-day'.

Gökotta (Sweden)
To go outside in the morning with the purpose of hearing the birds sing.

Harkla (Sweden)
A verb, meaning to clear your throat.

Hils (Sweden, Norway, Denmark)
Literally, 'greeting'. If someone is leaving your house to go home and you know the people they are going home to, you might say '*hils*'. It's a verb. Say '*hälsa*' in Sweden.

Ildsjel (Norway)
A fire soul – the person who runs everything, never runs out of energy, and never asks for anything in return (for the greater good of the community).

Klämdag (Sweden)
Literally, 'squeeze day'. If a holiday falls on a Thursday, the Friday is a 'squeeze day' in the sense that you will likely squeeze in an extra day off.

Köttrymd (Sweden)
This literally means 'the meat space', referring to a non-digital world.

Mambo (Sweden)
A Swede who lives with their mother is called a *mambo* – '*bo*' means to live somewhere. A *sambo* is living with your partner ('*sam*' = *sammen* = together).

Orke (Sweden, Norway, Denmark)
Orke is a verb that refers to not having the energy to do something.

Övermorgen (Sweden, Norway, Denmark)
The day after tomorrow, literally 'over tomorrow'.

Overskud (Denmark)
Literally, 'excess energy' or 'excess overview'.

Pålæg, pålegg (Sweden, Norway, Denmark)
Anything you can put on top of a slice of bread. Not the same as toppings.

Påtår (Sweden)
Refill of your coffee – and always coffee. A third one will be called *tretår* (three fills).

Pyt (Denmark)
Literally, 'puddle'. Can also be used as an 'it doesn't matter' word – as in '*Pyt* with that, we'll fix it some other way.'

Snälla (Sweden)
A version of 'kindly', 'sweetly'; a word that replaces the lack of the word 'please'. Only works in Swedish. In Danish and Norwegian, you would use the word *tak* ('thank you'), in place of 'please', although it is not always used in the same context.

Snuskhummer (Sweden)
The word refers to a dirty old man/pervert, but, literally, means 'dirty lobster'.

Tanketorsk (Denmark)
Literally, 'thought cod'. A gaffe, something you said without thinking about the consequences.

Utepils (Norway)
Literally, 'outside beer', this is the beer you have when you are sitting outside – the outside beer.

Paying taxes with a smile

If you look at it in a bit more detail, high taxes do not feel so scary, especially if you wear your Scandi hat and remember that underpinning everything we do is this overriding sense of 'togetherness' and 'for the best of the group'. While each of the three countries has its own specific rules and regulations, broadly taxes are high – very high. Sweden's top tax is around 59.7 per cent, with Denmark coming in second at 51.95 per cent, and Norway around 46 per cent. These include pension contributions and pretty much everything else. 'Tax' in Scandinavian languages is called *skat*. This is a word that also means 'treasure'. So, all the money for the greater good that is pooled into the pot, the treasure, that gives enough to make things work.

The systems are not the easiest to navigate, but suffice to say most Scandinavians, once everything is paid and said and done, will have a reasonable disposable income – at least 'quite sufficient'. What is left when the rich are taxed to the max is a large, broad middle class that – by and large – have similar spending power. Very few are truly poor or truly rich and the class system becomes a lot less defined.

What a lot of non-Scandis find peculiar is that, if you ask a Scandinavian person, he or she is generally unlikely to be particularly upset about the higher taxes. The level of income is higher – minimum wages set by either state or unions are in force, and everybody is looked after when it comes to working conditions.

While no system is perfect, the Scandinavian welfare model does provide basics in healthcare, pensions, unemployment, education and pretty much everything else to ensure the individual's needs are met. This ensures the group as a whole is happy and provided for. Rather than spend your own net income on expensive extra provisions for your health, children's education, pensions, etc., you pay for the basics upfront and can choose to add more, should you feel the need to. Sure, if you don't want children, and if you never get ill and you plan always to be in employment, you are paying for other people – and you might feel a bit miffed about it all. Mostly, though, it comes down to The Greater Good, the benefit for us all. Scandinavians are happy, generally, because they have their needs met and it is done in a fair way to all. As people often say: the reason Scandinavians are happy is not in spite of the high taxes, but partly because of them.

The happy bunch

While everything is slightly subjective and no two people's actual happiness can be the same, there are factors that make us all feel 'happy'. And since the seventies, Denmark, closely followed by other Nordic nations, loudly pings the top of the charts when it comes to happiness and general well-being.

People often ask why Scandinavian countries top these charts. Do we have a secret unicorn of happiness? Is there a magic pill, seeing as we take more antidepressants than other nations? Is it the *hygge*? Is it because we eat so much cake? Is it because we are happy being naked? The answer may lie in the fundamentals of human nature: having our basic needs met. Scandinavian countries are pretty good at spreading the wealth. Looking at Maslow's Hierarchy of Needs, these are met in abundance for most of us.

Generally, the societies in Scandinavia are built on *we*, rather than *I*. Families are looked after, the poor are looked after, the rich are taxed more and Mr Jensen next door may never be able to afford an expensive car, but that is ok, because Mr Jensen has been brought up knowing it is not necessary to strive for a Ferrari – it would only make the other people in town feel bad, anyway.

Because the welfare is solid, extreme poverty is reduced. We have not been to war for a long time (or even longer, if you are a Swede), so we have a feeling of safety. In general, you are likely to trust your neighbour, to leave the pram with your sleeping child outside the café. We know that our children are likely to get a free university education; we can afford to go to work because childcare is taken care of. Women and men are equal in their basic rights and, if you lose your job, you're unlikely to end up on the street. These factors all contribute to this overall happiness.

Then there are the elements of our home lives that contribute massively to this happiness. Scandinavians do not work long weeks. They leave the office on time and the kids – usually in day care all day – still get to spend a good amount of time with their parents.

And lastly, we're really good at *hygge*. To make time to do things together, leave the technology behind. To find that little space in our daily grind where only friends and family exist – the *hygge* spot, the *mys* spot, or *kos* – we're good at that. To appreciate the cake on the table, the glass of wine, the time spent with nice people. And maybe, just maybe, this is part of the secret: remembering the little comforts as being an essential part of life, not only striving for the Ferrari.

Superstitions

Old wives' tales and superstitions still reign today across Scandinavia. Everybody knows about not walking under a ladder, not putting new shoes on the table and not opening the umbrella indoors, but Scandinavians have a few of their own unique ones. Here are some of the best.

The number thirteen – Scandi version

In Norse mythology, twelve gods were invited to dine at the table in Valhalla. Loki, the mischievous god and shape-shifter, crashed the party and made it thirteen – and everything went to pieces. Lots of fighting. Baldr the Beautiful (god of joy and gladness) was killed with a mistletoe arrow because Loki made Hodr the Blind do it. As Christianity took hold in the centuries that followed the Vikings, the old Norse legends were reinforced in the form of the Last Supper, Jesus and Judas and thirteen at the table.

The black cat

In Scandinavia, a black cat is unlucky. In Sweden and Norway, if a black cat crosses your path, you have to spit three times to ward off evil spirits. An alternative is to just say '*tvi-tvi-tvi*' over your shoulder instead. It confuses Scandinavians when they go to Japan, where a black cat crossing your path means good luck.

A wonky slice of cake

In Denmark, if you cut a slice of cake and it falls on its side as you serve it, the recipient will end up with an all-round crazy mother-in-law. In Sweden, if the cake falls to the side as you accept it, you'll never get married. No amount of spitting will reverse the curses. Slightly contradictory if you put the two together. Either way, you'll either not get married or your life will be made hell by a bonkers mother-in-law. To avoid this horrid fate for your guests, simply use your fingers to help the cake stand upright until it reaches the table.

Touch wood

People all over the world like to touch wood to prevent bad things from happening or tempting fate. In Denmark, if you've said something to tempt fate, you knock three times under the table (*under*, never on) and say the numbers '*syv-ni-tretten*' ('seven-nine-thirteen') – one number per knock. It's a sort of double security with some lucky and some unlucky numbers in there. The number seven is thought to be lucky, nine is the number of worlds in old Norse mythology and thirteen is generally considered unlucky. In Sweden, people say '*Peppar, peppar ta i trä*' ('Pepper, pepper, knock on wood') to be extra-safe. Some say that the four 'p' sounds in '*Peppar, peppar*' can pacify the Devil, others that pepper was an expensive spice. Either way, always say it, or risk the consequences. The knock on wood/touch wood superstition has pagan origins, from the spirits and creatures who inhabited the woods – knocking on tree trunks would awaken them for protection.

Keys on the table

In Sweden, you must never put your keys on the table; it is considered very bad luck. Once you delve into the history of this, however, the origin of this superstition is that, back in the day, prostitutes used to indicate their availability by placing their keys on the table. After a while, it became bad luck to do so, seeing as people would not want to be thought of in that way. Even today, a Swede will hand you back your keys if you place them on the dining table.

Flags after sunset

In Denmark, if you forget to take the flag down from the flagpole in your garden, you're said to be raising the flag for the Devil.

Seven flowers under your pillow

On a Swedish Midsummer's Eve, pick seven different wild flowers and place them under your pillow. That night, you will dream of your true love. Or maybe you'll just dream about Liam Hemsworth. Maybe Liam Hemsworth *is* your true love, in which case, well done, flowers. If you don't have any wild flowers near you, pop down to your local corner shop and pick up a bunch of mixed carnations. It probably works just as well – it's the thought that counts, after all.

How to sneeze properly

Of course, you say '*prosit*' if someone sneezes. That goes without saying. In Denmark, if you sneeze once, it's good luck. Two times means you'll soon be kissed – and if you sneeze while tying your shoelaces, it's bad luck. Presumably this cancels out the good luck from one sneeze.

Break a leg

In Norway, instead of saying 'break a leg' , people say '*tvi-tvi*'.

Candles in the windows at Christmas

Across Scandinavia, you will find candles in the windows at Christmas. Of course, these are used to help guests find their way to your house in darkness but, in Denmark, they were believed to help spirits of deceased family members to find your house, too, as they were thought to visit at Christmas time.

Iron and knives by the door

Christmas opened up the doors not just for the spirits of your loved ones, but other creatures too, so many places in Denmark would add knives and iron bars above the door frame as they were thought to keep evil out of the house.

Whistling

In Denmark, never whistle on board a boat: you'll be calling a storm. If you whistle in the morning, you'll cry before evening. If you whistle in the evening, you're calling the Devil. Whistle just after dinner and you're saying thanks to the Devil, too. Whistling is pretty much not on, unless you're hunting for a four-leaf clover – in which case, you're all set.

Celebrations

Christmas in Scandinavia

Christmas is the most treasured time of the year. Picture the quaint houses, snow falling gently from the sky, landing like cottonwool on the cold landscape. Darkness may surround us in winter months, but in our hearts is so much warmth to fend off the cold outside. Every window has lights, towns are decorated tastefully. Real trees, candles everywhere, people wrapped up in seven layers of appropriate clothing walk arm in arm, into each other's houses to drink *glögg* and eat ginger biscuits. Sometimes...

The Vikings always celebrated the end of the year, the longest and darkest time, and how we celebrate it today goes right back to our forefathers and the old Norse rituals. The word *Jul*, which is what we call it, comes from the old Norse word *jól*. Interestingly, the name of the long-bearded god Odin bears the names *jólfaðr*, Old Norse for 'Yule father', and *jólnir*, 'the Yule one'; a sort of pagan version of a Santa, though less jolly ('jolly' is also a word that has roots in 'Yule', but that's a whole different story). Yule, or *Jul*, is also an old Germanic festive season that usually ran for around two months from mid-November to mid-January.

When King Haakon the Good of Norway, often credited with the Christianisation of Norway, came to power, he rescheduled the dates of *Jul* and the Christmas celebrations to coincide. He sold this new celebration to the very sceptical local Viking chiefs as a time when Christians and pagans could celebrate together and by law ordered everybody to celebrate as long as the

ale lasted. The new festive season was longer, thus more ale could be consumed. A positive suggestion, thought the chiefs, and drank some more. This is at the heart of what makes the Scandinavian Christmas so good – it's a celebration of the season, not a day on which you receive presents. The ale may have been swapped for *glögg*, but the spirit remains. Today, with fewer pagans and more Christians, Christmas has become a rich mixture of old and new traditions, of course with a bit of New World consumerism thrown into the mix.

The first sign of *Jul* in Scandinavia is Advent. The four Sundays before the big day are celebrated by all as the start of the season. Rarely do people buy presents or decorate before this day – usually at the very end of November. In fact, in Scandinavian countries in general decorations and the great hoo-ha is usually quite subdued until around the end of November.

Once the first Sunday in Advent comes around, so too does the *glögg* season. Scandinavian mulled wine is often made at home by the pot load, and shared with guests who pop by. It's a perfect way to make a cheap bottle of red wine into a culinary masterpiece, just by adding a bit of sugar and spices and heating it up. Serve with traditional ginger snaps and it is everybody's perfect tipple. It also has the bonus of keeping people warm – and it makes some people's ears and noses burn bright red, like *nisser*. There are non-alcoholic versions for drivers and kids as well.

No matter where you go, from north to south, you will be offered ginger biscuits in all shapes and sizes and regional variations. At Swedish and Norwegian *glögg* parties, you will most likely also be served *Lussebullar*, saffron-flavoured yeast buns (especially during the feast of St Lucia on 13 December). In Denmark, you will be served *Æbleskiver* pancake balls, dipped in icing sugar and jam.

Another sign that the time is near is the use of calendar candles (burn a little every day), chocolate advent calendars or – in some places – present calendars. Usually reserved for little kids, the presents are delivered by the *nisse/tomte* at night and placed in a stocking. In Norway, the gift calendars are less popular; Norwegians instead opt for little messages such as 'Tonight we go ICE SKATING!' because, well, Norwegians like to have excuses to get outdoors ... all the time.

Lucia

When 13 December rolls around, things go up a gear as people prepare for St Lucia. St Lucia is celebrated all over Scandinavia on 13 December (*Luciadagen*). The tradition has both Christian and pagan roots. Firstl it is the Feast of St Lucia of Syracuse (283–304). This day once coincided with the Winter Solstice, the shortest day in the year before calendar reforms, so St Lucia's feast day has now become a Festival of Light across Scandinavia. It's a great example of where our pagan heritage meets Christianity.

The old pagan *Lussinatt* was the darkest night when spirits, gnomes and trolls roamed the earth. Lussi, a feared enchantress, punished anyone who dared work. Legend also has it that farm animals talked to each other on this night. On this magical eve, we drive the evil spirits away with candles and singing in the darkness.

Nowadays, the celebrations start with processions, through every town, of girls and boys wearing white robes tied with red sashes, holding candles. At the front, usually a girl – the Lucia Bride – wears a wreath of real candles in her hair. The processions start on Lucia morning, in the darkness, and usually carry on until daylight breaks.

It is a truly magical experience to see a really good Lucia choir by candlelight. There is no better way to start the Christmas countdown and there is no way anyone can sit through a session of children singing Christmas carols, feeling tipsy from warm *glögg* at 10 a.m., and not feel festive.

Lussekatter – Lucia celebration saffron buns
Makes 12–15 buns

Ingredients
0.5 g saffron powder or a large pinch
   of saffron strands
200 ml (7 fl oz) whole milk
25 g (1 oz) fresh yeast or 15 g (½ oz)
   active, dry yeast
75 g (3 oz) caster sugar
½ teaspoon salt
Approximately 400–500 g (13 oz–1
   lb) plain bread flour, plus extra for
   dusting
100 ml (3½ fl oz) Greek yoghurt, at
   room temperature
1 egg
100 g (3½ oz) butter, softened
Handful of nice plump raisins

1. If using saffron strands, soak in the milk to make the milk a strong yellow colour.

2. Set up a stand mixer with a dough-hook attachment. Place the milk in a saucepan and heat to 37–38°C (98–100°F), which is finger-warm. If it is too hot, you'll kill the yeast, so do check it. If using dried yeast, take the milk off the heat, mix in the yeast and set the yeast mixture aside for 15 minutes to allow the yeast to activate. If using fresh yeast, add the milk and yeast to the mixer bowl. Mix until the yeast has dissolved, then add the saffron powder, if using powder.

3. Add the sugar and mix again for a minute. Mix the salt into the flour in a separate bowl, then add some of the flour mixture, the yoghurt and half the egg and mix well. Next, add the butter and gradually add the remainder of the flour while mixing. You'll need around 400 g (13 oz) of flour, but the exact amount depends on how the dough feels. Keep mixing until you have a dough that is still sticky, but doesn't stick to your finger too much when you poke it. Too much flour makes the buns dry and you can always add more flour after the proving.

4. If you're using an electric mixer, knead for about 5 minutes or knead by hand for 10 minutes. Cover the bowl with clingfilm and leave the dough to rise in a warm place for about 30–40 minutes, until doubled in size.

5. Turn the dough out onto a lightly floured surface and knead for about 5 minutes, using just enough flour that you're able to work with the dough. Cut the dough into 12–15 equal-sized pieces. Roll each piece in your hand into a long cylinder, then transfer to a lined baking tray and mould into an 'S' shape. Leave to rise again for 25 minutes.

6. Preheat the oven to 200°C (400°F, Gas Mark 6). Add a single raisin to the centre of where the 'S' shape curves (two raisins for each bun), then brush gently with the remaining egg and bake for 10–12 minutes. The buns should have a slight tinge of brown on top, but

not too much – you may need to turn the heat down if they start to brown, to ensure they remain a strong yellow colour.

7. Remove from the oven and cover with a clean, slightly dampened tea towel to prevent the buns drying out. Enjoy in December, especially on Sundays in Advent, with a warming mug of *glögg*.

The big day

If you want to celebrate Christmas the Scandi way, only a real tree will do . Also, in Denmark, you decorate it with real candles that you will light on Christmas Eve. You then have exactly sixteen minutes while they burn to gather the family, hold hands and run around the tree, singing carols at the top of your panic-stricken, fire-alert voice. It is most amusing to walk around a Danish town at around 8 p.m. on Christmas Eve to witness this in every window.

Christmas Eve is the main occasion for celebrations. Some say that one of the reasons Christmas is celebrated on Christmas Eve rather than Christmas Day is because the Vikings believed a new day began when the other one ended – so, at sundown. There is no proof to back this up and also it doesn't explain why it is the same in most of Germany and other Protestant countries. But it's a nice thought. And true, indeed, that everything happens on Christmas Eve.

A typical Christmas Eve is spent preparing the food throughout the day. Different countries have slightly different traditions in terms of food – the Swedes will have a full-on smörgåsbord, whereas the Danes and Norwegians will have warm meals of a more comfort-food nature. Churchgoers will head to church in the afternoon and others will spend the day decorating the tree (in some areas, this is not done until the last moment), wrapping the final presents and getting the house ready for the evening's festivities. To Norwegians, the 3 p.m. ringing of bells is the sign that it is Christmas; whether they go to church or not, this is when Christmas starts.

In Sweden, everything starts mid-afternoon when an old TV re-run of *Walt Disney Presents Christmas* is shown on prime-time telly (more than half the Swedish population watches *Kalle Anka och hans vänner önskar God Jul*). Every year, this show is screened at the same time. The same show, from the fifties, with new bits added each year and old bits removed. It signals the start of the evening and time to sit down and eat. In Norway and Denmark, the same show is also broadcast, although with fewer rules attached. In Norway, a repeat of an old seventies Czech movie called in Norwegian, *Three Nuts for Cinderella* is shown. It is a dubbed version, in the cruellest form possible: the sound turned down on the original speech, one man dubbing all the voices in Norwegian. It's very popular and nobody knows why.

Later on, the *nisse* or *tomte* will visit and bring presents. Usually, he looks a bit like your Uncle Henrik. Maybe Uncle Henrik is the forgotten half-son of an elf? One never knows; they look alike anyway.

Once the rest of the presents have been opened, the kids will spend the evening playing and, seeing as the children have no bedtime that day, the adults will slowly consume whatever alcoholic beverages they can find. Then they'll have some coffee to perk themselves up before ending the evening before midnight.

Christmas Day is the start of the family *smörgåsbord* get-togethers – the next two or three days are spent visiting people, eating leftovers and drinking more aquavit. More *glögg*, more ginger biscuits. By this point, most start dreaming of healthy salads.

When New Year's Eve comes around, people will get together with friends, have parties, like most others around the world do. Every person will watch the king or queen's speech on telly and every person will be forced to sit through a ten-minute repeat of the old British TV sketch called *Dinner for One*. Broadcast every year on Scandinavian TV since time began, it will continue to be shown every year until Ragnarök. Everybody laughs. Not because they have to, but because it's bloody funny. This sketch epitomises everything about Scandinavian New Year and humour in one, however odd this might sound.

There are fireworks and fancy food and, at midnight, as the bells ring in the New Year, Danes will jump down from chairs onto the floor, as is traditional. Nobody else has this tradition, but Danes across the world will do this and will always expect to be taken seriously, so you'd better join them in jumping into the New Year. Same procedure as last year. Every year. Tradition is a wonderful, wonderful thing.

In Denmark and Norway, you have to get rid of your tree by 6 January. In Sweden, it is much later – one month after Lucia, on 13 January – and there is a whole post-Christmas let's-do-it-again thing where you have to dance around the tree and you get another present, and then you carry the tree out of the house and to an appropriate recycling place. And so, finally, Christmas has ended and we start to look forward to Easter and the lighter days.

15 steps to Christmas the Scandi way

1. Get excited.
2. Don't start making Christmas plans until the last weekend of November.
3. Find a way to make snow.
4. Wear layers and jumpers when out in cold weather.
5. Replace Santa with the little *nisser/tomter*. You don't need the big man when you have the little elves.
6. Celebrate Sundays in Advent like a true Scandi and get *glögg*-making.
7. Overdo the little candles and lights. Everywhere, on every surface. Fairy lights are acceptable, but only if they are a tasteful warm white. It is all about creating the atmosphere of a snowy, cottage hideaway. If you have no log fire and don't fancy setting your sofa alight, try to create that cottage feel in other ways – think more lamps, blankets, bowls of whole nuts, oranges, spiced biscuits.
9. Decorate tastefully. Scandinavians are not plastic and glittery tinsel appreciators. To work out if something is Scandi enough: Is it made of wood, old, looks like it belongs in a cottage? Is it made by a designer, does it have sleek and uninterrupted lines? Does it feature a little troll or elf wearing a red hat? Any of these means you're good to go. If it has the word 'glitter' or 'magic Christmas sounds' on the packaging, throw it away.
10. Bring nature indoors. Get the smell of Christmas not only from your real tree, but also from the logs for the fire. Don't have a log fire? Bring some wood in anyway. Or some twigs. Or just fir-tree branches if you don't have space for the tree. Do get a real tree. It does not have to be big – just real.
11. Celebrate St Lucia on 13 December like a pro.
12. Bake: ginger biscuits, gingerbread houses, buns, any cakes containing marzipan, seven kinds of biscuits other than ginger, breads and more. For the love of Odin, just bake something, people.
13. Watch *Walt Disney Presents Christmas* at 3 p.m., on the dot, on Christmas Eve.
14. Celebrate the big day on Christmas Eve instead of Christmas Day. At home or with family – never, *ever* go to the pub on Christmas Eve, that is simply unacceptable.
15. If you can still stomach it, spend 25 and 26 December finishing off the last of the *glögg*, visiting friends and eating their leftovers.

God Jul.

Glögg
Makes 6–7 glasses

Ingredients
A bottle of red wine

Dried Seville orange peel

Stick of cinnamon

5g (¼ oz) whole dried ginger

10 whole cloves

20 whole cardamom pods

80 g (3 oz) sugar

1 teaspoon flaked almonds (per glass)

1 teaspoon raisins (per glass)

Dash of brandy (optional)

1. In a saucepan, gently heat the red wine, sugar, peel and spices to 80°C (176°F). Don't let it boil or the alcohol will evaporate. Take off the heat and leave to infuse for at least an hour. Remove the spices and peel.

2. When ready to serve, gently reheat and serve in small cups, topped with the almonds and raisins and a dash of brandy if it's really cold outside.

Fat Tuesday and semlor

Lent in Scandinavia is a big thing, celebrated slightly differently in the various countries. In Denmark and some parts of Norway, the main celebration takes place on the Monday before Ash Wednesday. This day is known as *Fastelavn* – the Lutheran word for 'carnival'. The word actually comes from old Danish – *fastelaghen* – meaning the 'fast evening'. This day is celebrated by children mostly, who dress up in fancy dress and sometimes go door to door and beg for coins or sweets, not dissimilar to trick-or-treating.

Another slightly more macabre tradition on this day is *'slå katten af tønden'* – literally 'beat the cat out of the barrel'. This is a large barrel, stuffed with sweets and goodies and decorated with streamers and pictures of black cats. In true piñata-style, it is then hung up. Children take turns to beat the barrel with a bat until it breaks. Up until the late 1890s, it was still traditional to put a live black kitten into the barrel, too – it was thought the beating of the barrel would also beat the evil out of the creature.

After the barrel has broken, a Cat King and Cat Queen will be crowned from among the kids – the biggest honour of them all. Usually, the King and Queen are chosen based on the originality of their costumes.

Another even more ancient tradition is the Danish and southern Swedish tradition of *Fastelavnsris*: a bouquet of budding birch twigs decorated with colourful paper, sweets and feathers. These were traditionally used to whip the young maidens of the village, who could then 'buy' their way out of further amorous whipping advances by offering some Shrovetide buns to the young gentlemen. Today in Denmark, no maidens are whipped, but the tradition of the decorated twigs lives on, with kids using them to wake their parents on *Fastelavn* morning.

The tradition of birch twigs as a fertility symbol stems from olden times. Another such fifteenth-century fertility ritual was for the farm boys to run around the field naked while sowing seeds, with the ladies looking on from the sidelines, hiking up their skirts to show their bare buttocks. Rumour has it this still happens in some places in Jutland on Friday evenings.

Shrove Tuesday is the biggest day in Sweden and Norway. Also known as Fat Tuesday – *Fettisdagen* – this is the day when people fatten up before Lent, which starts on Ash Wednesday. On this day, buns stuffed with cream, jam and/or marzipan are enjoyed by all – and you can eat as many as you want. These buns are known in Sweden as *semla* (plural: *semlor*). In Norway and Denmark they are known as *Fastelavnsboller* (Lent buns).

A *semla* is a heavy wheat bun, the top quarter of which is sliced off to form a lid. The insides are hollowed out, mixed with marzipan and a bit of milk and this is then used to fill the hollow. Whipped cream is then piped on top and the lid replaced, after which the whole thing is dusted with icing sugar. In Sweden especially, people form queues at the bakers to get their hands on their stash of buns. It used to be tradition that the buns were only sold on Shrove Tuesday, but nowadays shops start selling them as early as January. In fact, there used to be a law governing when these buns could be made and sold, and if shops served them outside of those dates, they could – and would – be fined. Even today, no one sells *semla* buns from after Easter until Christmas – it is just never done. The average Swede eats around five *semlor* per person during the season, whereas the Norwegians and Danes eat a lot fewer. This is the one day of the year in Sweden when *lagom* does not apply.

Semlor are not a recent thing – it has been a huge part of Swedish culinary history for centuries. King Adolf Fredrik, ruler of Sweden 1751–71, reputedly died from eating fourteen *semlor* in one sitting. He is affectionately referred to as the King Who Ate Himself to Death. Admittedly, he also had a full-on banquet, including lobster, caviar and Champagne before his excessive bun-eating. He died of terrible indigestion that same night. A grisly end, but a sweet one.

Semlor (Swedish Lent buns)
Makes 12 generous buns

For the buns

120 g (3½ oz) butter
240 ml (7¾ fl oz) whole milk
25 g (1 oz) fresh yeast or 13 g (½ oz)
  active dry yeast
50 g (2 oz) caster sugar
Approximately 400–500 g (13 oz–1lb)
  plain bread flour, plus extra for
  dusting
½ teaspoon salt
1 teaspoon baking powder
2–3 teaspoons ground cardamom (if
  fresh, use less; if older, use more –
  you need a good, strong flavour)
1 egg, lightly beaten

Filling

100 g (3½ oz) good-quality marzipan
A good dollop of thick custard, milk or
  crème pâtissière
500 ml (17 fl oz) whipping cream
1 teaspoon vanilla sugar
Icing sugar, to dust

1. Set up the stand mixer with a dough-hook attachment. Place the butter in a saucepan and melt gently. Add the milk, ensuring a lukewarm temperature of 37–38°C (98–100°F).

2. If the milk mixture is too hot the yeast will die, so do measure. Take the milk mixture off the heat. Add the yeast and stir until dissolved. If using dried yeast, set the milk and yeast mixture aside for 15 minutes to allow the yeast to activate.

3. Add sugar and stir again. Pour the milk mixture into the mixer bowl. Add half of the flour with the salt, baking powder and ground cardamom and mix. Add half the beaten egg (keep the rest for brushing).

4. Mix well until all ingredients are incorporated and then start to add more of the flour, bit by bit, until you have a dough that is only slightly sticky. Take care not to add too much flour or you will get dry buns – nobody likes dry buns.

5. Knead the dough for at least 5 minutes. Cover and leave to rise in a warm (not hot) place, for about 30–40 minutes, until doubled in size.

6. Turn the dough out onto a lightly floured surface. Knead again for a few minutes, adding more flour if needed. Cut the dough into 12 equal-sized pieces and roll into very uniform-sized buns.

7. Place on a baking tray with good spacing between buns. Covered, leave to rise for another 25–30 minutes.

8. Preheat the oven to 190°C Fan/200°C (400°F, Gas Mark 6). Gently brush each bun with the remainder of the beaten egg and bake for 8–10 minutes. Keep an eye on them as they can burn quickly because of the sugar content.

9. Remove from the oven and immediately cover the tray with a lightly dampened, clean tea towel. This will prevent the buns from forming a crust.

10. When they have cooled down completely, slice a lid off the buns, about a quarter from the top. Scoop out about one-third of the inside of each bun and place in a bowl. Add the marzipan and mix until it forms a very sticky mass. Add a dash of milk, custard or crème pâtissière at this point to help it along. You want a spoonable, even mixture. Spoon the filling back into the buns. Whip the cream with the vanilla sugar until stiff, then use a piping bag to pipe cream on top of the buns. Put the lids back on and dust lightly with icing sugar.

11. The buns freeze well without the filling and cream but once filled, should be eaten on the same day.

How to eat a *semla*

As it is, holding it in your hand. You will get cream on your nose. Use the lid to scoop off and eat some of the cream first, making it easier to eat the bun. Add the bun to a bowl and pour in hot milk, a bit like when you're having cereal in the morning. Eat with a spoon, like a dessert. This version is called *hetvägg* and it is the only way some purists will eat it. A knife and fork will also work.

Easter in Scandinavia

After the long, dark months lit almost entirely by candles and streetlamps, the light finally breaks across Scandinavia and people wake from hibernation. The ground starts to thaw and there is once more a bit of daylight when you leave the office and when you wake in the mornings. Along rolls Eastertime and a nice long holiday break across Scandinavia signals the winter is finally ready to come to an end. The forest once again has green buds, the ground is awake with activity and the pace of life picks up after the slow giant of the long winter.

Across Sweden, people finally stop eating the *semla* cream buns they have been enjoying since Fat Tuesday. Like elsewhere across the Western world, Easter is all about the chicks, eggs and chocolate. It's about family time, good food, good company and a break from work and is usually a chance to leave the towns and cities for a bit of an injection of Mother Nature. This is high season for *hytter* – the cabins and summer houses most Scandinavians love so much.

Sweden, Denmark and Norway share a lot of the Easter traditions, of course, going back both to pagan times and Christianity. Easter is known as *Påsk* (*Påske*), a word stemming from the Hebrew *Pesach*, or Passover. By 1200 AD, the Norse people were mixing their own traditions with religious ones and still today a lot of the old rituals have happily married with the Christian ones. For example, in Sweden, the Norse people would collect the bare winter branches and burn them as part of a celebration to ward off evil spirits and today, although slightly later than Easter, on the night of 30 April, bonfires are made and burned all across Sweden on what is known as *Valborgsmässoafton* (Walpurgis Night).

The family get-togethers and the religious aspect all come into play, but despite us celebrating the same thing, each country has very unique traditions, too.

Sweden has Easter celebrations that are deeply rooted in the old Christian witch-hunt times. These celebrations last from Maundy Thursday until Easter Monday. In the olden days it was thought that on Maundy Thursday all the witches would fly off on their broomsticks to the Blue Mountains (*Blåkulla*) in Germany to have a weekend of fun and dancing with Satan (this same belief is mirrored in the Danish St John's Eve celebration a few months later).

Today, children in Sweden celebrate by dressing up as little witches, called *påskkärringar* (literally, 'Easter witches'), in long skirts and headscarves, with painted-on red cheeks and freckles. The kids go from house to house to collect coins and far too many sweets. This is the Swedish version of the North American tradition of Halloween and is also mirrored in the Danish and Norwegian *fastelavn*, where kids do this on Maundy Monday. The children

sometimes also deliver an Easter letter – the identity of the sender is always supposed to be a secret.

In Sweden you often see decorated birch twigs around this time. The use of birch is a symbol of spiritual renewal and people would gather them and place them in water then wait for the buds to come out, signifying renewal and rebirth. In the 1900s people started decorating them with colourful feathers and little eggs. These birch bouquets are known as *påskris*.

In Norway, a slightly different tradition is associated with Easter, with no links to anything much historic. Around Easter, publishers rush to churn out masses of what are known to all Norwegians as *Påskekrimmen* – literally translated, these are 'Easter thrillers' – and bookshops are filled with newly published crime novels. Most crime novels in Norway are published around this time of the year. The TV schedules are full of Easter crime series, all hotly debated and reviewed, and most Easter holidays in Norway are spent visiting the *hytte* in the mountains, seizing the chance for the last few skiing trips and lots of relaxing reading time about murders.

This fascination with whodunnits even extends to mini-thrillers being published in obscure places. Tine, the milk producer in Norway, have a mini-series on the side of milk cartons every year.

In Denmark, the tradition of writing 'teaser letters' (*gækkebreve*) still holds strong and has done since the early 1800s. A teaser letter is a pattern carefully cut into a piece of paper with a little verse written between the cuts. The sender adds dots in place of his or her name and encloses a snowdrop flower – considered to be the first flower of the year in Denmark and a symbol of springtime and lighter days. Off goes the letter. If the recipient cannot guess before Easter who sent the letter, the prize for the sender is a nice, big Easter egg. If, however, the recipient guesses, the prize goes to the recipient (although, miraculously, most parents never do seem to be able to guess which letters are from their own kids). A famous verse to include in your cutting:

Gæk, gæk, gæk – mit navn det står med prikker pas på det ikke stikker

('Trick, trick, trick – my name is written with dots, careful they don't sting you')

The word *gæk* is synonymous with 'fun' – and the snowdrop flower is known as a *vintergæk* flower.Easter concludes with a massive Easter *smörgåsbord* for the family, usually with a few added fish and egg dishes to reflect the seasonality.

How to ... Eurovision

Once a year, the Eurovision Song Contest takes place somewhere in Europe (or thereabouts). It's a contest where lots of countries compete to win best song. Set up in 1956 to promote happy feelings between European countries after the war, and now over sixty years old, it is an orgy of glitter, confetti and sequins. There is also some music.

To enjoy Eurovision like a Scandi you must go into full *Fredagsmys* (Cosy Friday), even if it's on a Saturday. It's one of the few times of the year that Cosy Friday is moved to a Saturday. On Eurovision night, you are allowed both crisps and sweets – and also cocktails, if it's the final.

While the popularity of the Eurovision Song Contest has nosedived in many countries, in others, such as Denmark and Norway, it has remained popular, and in some, like Sweden, its popularity has sky-rocketed. In Sweden, they host six regional heats to find the winning song that will represent king and country at the big final. In most countries, they manage to choose a song in one evening. After the regional heats, a winner is chosen. Arenas are filled with happy people, there is laughter and singsong, wind machines and cleavages. There are also awkward dance moves that would rival your Uncle Henrik's. The song will hit the top of the Swedish charts and people start to look forward to the big event a few months later.

In recent years, Sweden has started winning more and more. In the years between Swedish wins, Norway or Denmark may win. Now Sweden thinks it can win every year and so as not to disappoint the people back home, they make sure most of the other countries use Swedish producers, singers, writers, dancers or ukulele players. If you look, you will see a Swedish connection in most of the acts, ensuring Sweden sort of always wins.

Eurovision in Scandinavia is still rife with voting for your neighbours. The rules keep changing to avoid neighbour voting, but, somehow, Sweden and Denmark will still give each other top points; the rest will be dished out to Norway, Iceland and a point or two for Finland. Sometimes we vote because we like the song. Sometimes it's the wind machines or the political message. We do like a good political message, mainly because it's not allowed.

You can't talk about Eurovision without talking about ABBA, the most famous Swedish winners of all time. In 1974, they sang about Waterloo and they won the whole contest. That was the year the UK gave Sweden *nul points*, which may be why the UK never wins nowadays because the Swedish ScWager mafia is in charge.

ABBA went on to be one of the biggest bands in the world. There is no family party or disco without at least one or two Dancing Queens. Sweden is so proud of ABBA that there is even a museum dedicated to them. It's a lesser-known fact that ABBA took their name from a brand of pickled herring – it had no known influence on their music.

Norwegian National Day

Norwegians win the prize for having the most elaborate and festive national day of Scandinavia, hands down. Every year on *Søttende Mai* (17 May), the entire country, along with Norwegians around the world, will spend the day celebrating and feeling patriotic. On this day, if you are anywhere near a Norwegian, you will see more flags than you thought possible. It's impossible not to be swept away by armies of happy Norwegians, beaming from ear to ear.

In 1814, after centuries under rule by both Sweden and Denmark, Norway got its own constitution, signed on 17 May. Initially, the Norwegians were not allowed to celebrate – in fact, it was forbidden – as they were officially still in union with Sweden but by 1833 a public address was held on 17 May and the first parades began in the 1860s. The union was officially dissolved in 1905, ending any concerns the Swedes could voice about the celebrations.

On the 17 May, everybody has parades. In all towns, virtually any club with more than one member will join a parade. From sewing clubs, schools, dentists and veterans to Harley-Davidson clubs. Those who do not join the parade line the streets with flags and wave excessively as they look around, hoping to catch a glimpse of someone they know.

Most people will begin the day with a Champagne breakfast at home or at a friends' or family member's house. It happens early (around 7 a.m.) so that people can get to the parades. This is a *koldtbord* (*smörgåsbord*) consisting of scrambled egg, air-dried lamb, prawns, salmon, roast beef, cheese, fruit salad, *rømmegrøt* (sour cream porridge), fresh bread and lashings of wine and Champagne. It is likely the most abundant meal of the year, often bigger than the Christmas meal, with no expense spared. Once you get out to the parades, hotdogs and ice cream are the important things to source. Tables for breakfast, lunch or dinner in a restaurant need to be booked well in advance (it is impossible to get a spot to eat otherwise) so most people eat hotdogs, ice cream and waffles from vendors and cafés throughout the day.

On *Søttende Mai*, anyone who has a *bunad* will wear it. A *bunad* is traditional Norwegian dress, made of very heavy wool. Those who own one will wear it come rain or shine. They are handmade and cost £3,500–7,500 each, so best get some wear out of it. Most people love wearing their *bunad*, especially for the first two hours. After this, it can become hard work, particularly if the weather doesn't play fair.

The *bunad* has been around since the late 1800s. Each valley has its own design, but some people pick the one they like the best. A *bunad* is also acceptable gala attire, so if you are invited to visit the king, you'd likely wear your *bunad*. People also get married wearing one.

The *bunad* has lots of signifiers. For example, the length of your skirt can denote whether or not you are married, as does the special silver decoration on the men's belts. Some *bunad* have matching hats called *kyse*.

Not being able to do up the *bunad* can be a recurring annual issue. A lot of people receive their *bunad* as a gift when they are fifteen or sixteen years old, and it does not allow for expanding waistlines or ageing ungracefully. Rubber bands are often used when buttons will not close. On the flipside, sometimes they are bought very big, so some people look around 10 kg (22 lb) heavier than they really are. It's a special look.

After a day of eating ice cream and waving flags, a lot of people will hit the dance floor. Some will do this wearing their *bunad*. This practice is often referred to as *bunadsboogie*. It is not recommended as it is hot, uncomfortable and itchy. Also, you're wearing old-fashioned shoes and likely over-decorated with silver buckles.

The celebrations last the whole day with festive music – some traditional bands and some less so – playing at the events and town centres. The evening will finish with dinner and then up for work the next morning. Unless, of course, you get tempted by a late-night *bunadsboogie*.

While 17 May is a public holiday, the day after is not, so some people do their evening celebration on the 16th, or some call in sick on the 18th, thinking they are going to get away with the 'I had some bad chicken last night' excuse. The rate of people calling in sick on 18 May is extremely high in Norway.

Danish National Day

Denmark is a very proud little country. Proud of the flag, proud of the landscape, proud of the history. You might think they'd have the biggest national day celebration of all, but no.

Danish National Day isn't really a national day, but a constitution day – the Danes do not have a national day as such, so this is the closest they get to one. It's a celebration of the anniversary of the signing of the Danish Constitution which established Denmark as a constitutional monarchy on 5 June 1849. The day is known as *Grundlovsdag* (Constitution Day).

Since the signing of the first Constitution, some amendments have been made – in 1915 when women got the right to vote and again in 1953, when the voting age was lowered and royal male and female heirs were given equal rights to the throne. All amendments happened on the same date of 5 June. In 1935, this also became Father's Day – a new tradition imported from America – which is now always celebrated on 5 June in Denmark.

The day in Denmark is a public holiday, but with some exceptions. This causes confusion at times. Most shops are closed, some official buildings and public offices are closed all day, but some only close for half the day. Some places of work are open, some are closed, others have a half day. Many, but not all, schools and some nurseries are closed.

Grundlovsdag in Denmark is usually a day for political speeches and rallies, as well as for some patriotic celebrations, and some people even meet up for singsongs of the national anthem and other traditional songs, but mostly it is a calm affair. The public buildings will fly the flag and most certainly Danes walk a little taller, but that's about it: don't plan your visit around it or anything.

Swedish National Day

You could be forgiven for thinking Midsummer is Sweden's National Day. A day of flowers, Swedish flags, traditional dress, songs about wonderful Sweden and being at one with nature and aquavit. But no, the official Swedish National Day is a few weeks earlier, on 6 June. For years and years, Sweden didn't have a national day and several attempts to create one fell flat.

From 1892, however, *Svenska flaggans dag* was created to celebrate the Swedish flag on 6 June. Gustav Vasa, King of Sweden, was crowned on 6 June 1523. In 1809, on the same day, the king's right to absolute rule was ended, and this was the start of the Swedish democratisation and constitution. In 1916, 6 June became the Swedish Flag Day. This day remained just a day at Skansen (Stockholm's open-air museum) when the flag was celebrated, but not many in the rest of the country paid much attention to it.

In 1983, after much debate, it was decided 6 June should be the new National Day, the Day of the Flag. It continued to be a normal working day until 2005, when it was finally made a 'red day', a public holiday.

Every year on 6 June the Swedish royal family attend National Day celebrations at Skansen and blue and yellow flags are displayed everywhere. It is also a day when new Swedish people join the country. The national anthem (not 'Dancing Queen') is sung, and people revel in national pride, the *lagom* way.

Seeing as National Day is now a holiday, people are off work and school. The day can be celebrated with a nice family dinner, flags in the garden, a singsong, but not much else. Some towns have National Day events but nothing is as big as Midsummer a few weeks later and everybody saves their energy for the bigger day. As 6 June is so close to Midsummer, it is hard to separate the two.

Midsummer in Scandinavia

Midsummer, to Swedes especially, is one of the biggest celebrations of the year. In Sweden, the date moves each year, as it is an official holiday – and it is always celebrated on a Friday. With the official midsummer day of the year being 23 June, it is always moved to the closest Friday (for 2017, this is 23 June, 22 June for 2018 and 21 June for 2019). In Denmark and Norway, the date doesn't move – it is always celebrated on the evening of 23 June. In Sweden, *Midsommar* is simply known as that, whereas in Denmark and Norway the name has changed to *St Hans Aften* ('St John's Eve'). That's the official name, although it's also known as *Midsommer*.

As the longest day of the year, midsummer was a very important day in the pagan calendar. The Vikings used this night to visit healing water wells and had huge bonfires to ward off evil spirits. These celebrations go back to Freyia and Freyr, the Norse gods of fertility. The Vikings worshipped fertility on this day – and hoped for a rich harvest.

Today, you see the remains of these old traditions both in Sweden and Denmark. Sweden's midsummer symbol is now a midsummer pole, *Midsommarstång*, decorated with flowers. (It was originally a Maypole, likely brought over from Germany, but there weren't enough flowers to decorate it in May so it is now used in June instead.) In Denmark and Norway, the bonfires won out and are still the main symbol of midsummer. Schools and offices close and it is the time for friends and families to get together. People wear flower garlands in their hair; some wear traditional dresses or just long, light-coloured dresses. Younger men wear traditional clothing for Swedish dudes: light-coloured, tight trousers, pointy shoes, sunglasses and slicked-back hair. Maybe a crown of flowers.

The flower garlands are a major part of the outfit. Most people make their own while sitting in a field, waiting to celebrate. People gather wild flowers and the garlands are made for grown-ups as well as children. This adds to the picture-perfect setting – everything becomes wonderfully colourful and happy, as people sit in nature and enjoy the lightest day of the year. Thus properly attired, they gather to raise the midsummer pole, which is decorated with more flowers and leaves and can be anything from small poles in private gardens to massive poles in the town centres.

Where food is concerned, everybody brings a picnic or has a midsummer lunch together. Lunch always consists of pickled herring, new potatoes with dill, meatballs, cheese... Not dissimilar to food at other Swedish celebrations, but with a lot more strawberries, as these are usually just in season when midsummer comes around. This is also a big day for *smörgåstårta*. With this, people enjoy aquavit, in shots (*nubbe*). Roughly one shot to every two beers.

Drinking songs, such as '*Helan går*', are sung, shots are enjoyed and after a few of those, almost everybody will feel ready to dance. Don't worry if you can't sing songs in Swedish, after two or three *nubbar*, people automatically develop a singsong fluency in Swedish. The party then gathers around the midsummer pole to hold hands and starts to run around in circles, pretending to be little frogs with no ears and tail. This is the traditional Swedish song – sung at every party – called '*Små grodarna*' (the 'Little Frogs'). If you are ever invited to join in, you must oblige. It would be rude not to and nobody feels embarrassed about this dance. Once it's over, you'll be allowed to get back to more food and aquavit. The afternoon is usually spent playing games. When people have finished eating and playing, the dancing continues – as does the drinking. The party will go on until last man standing, with darkness never setting on this lightest day of the year.

On this night, it is also tradition to pick seven different kinds of wild flowers. Put them under your pillow before going to bed and you will dream of the person you will marry. This makes Tinder-swiping a whole lot easier as you will now know what he or she looks like.

In Denmark and Norway, people are a little more controlled in their midsummer celebrations. It is not a public holiday and, while it is still a big celebration, it is by no means as big as in Sweden. The celebrations centre around big bonfires, usually by the shore or in town centres. Bonfires, originally intented to ward off evil spirits, have become slightly warped in Denmark over the years. Nowadays, they signify the burning of witches. Each bonfire has a witch made out of straw, dressed in old ladies' clothing and stuffed with whistle crackers. The fire is lit and everybody waits for the witch to catch fire, the whistles signifying her screams. Legend has it that, by doing this, you send the witch off to the Brocken mountain in Germany to dance with the Devil.

As they watch the witch burn, people sing songs about how much they love Denmark. There is usually a guy with a guitar and no socks. He plays songs slowly, with his eyes closed. There may or may not be skinny dipping. At midsummer in Denmark, kids will usually be making *snobrød* ('twist bread'). The fire ends and people go home. Unlike Sweden, this isn't a massive party, but a much calmer affair (save the burning of witches, of course; some may find this rather sinister).

From the dancing and the ancient traditions to the seasonal food and togetherness, Midsummer in Scandinavia is an enchanted time and writing about it doesn't do it full justice. The light is entirely spellbinding – and it's something to be experienced.

The day after Midsummer in Sweden, in particular, is a whole different ball game – and it's yours alone to deal with. The 'where are my shoes?' questions will inevitably start to be pondered on. Who are you? Who am I? For anyone who has partaken of a traditional Swedish Midsummer, the day after is likely to be long – and very slow. But you'll always have the memories. Or not.

The crayfish season

Every year in August, Swedes get super-excited by the start of the crayfish season. Back in the 1800s, Napoleon developed a thing for *écrevisses*, and people on the rest of the continent followed suit. Crayfish became all the rage and the craze even spread to the Nordic countries, where a natural abundance of these little creatures made them easy to come by. As the gastronomic trend spread, stocks started to decline, and a lethal pest some decades later almost wiped out the entire European stock. After this, the Swedish government imposed a strict crayfish fishing season and, from this, the tradition of crayfish season, in the month of August, was born.

Nowadays there isn't really a legal season, but Swedes do like tradition and rules, so no self-respecting Swede will host a crayfish party (*kräftskiva*) other than in August. Every July, all newspapers run full-page 'Best in Test' articles, revealing which of the various retail crayfish companies has produced the best stock that year. Most crayfish is farmed and imported from across the globe to satisfy the huge demand. It's not unusual to attend two or three crayfish parties in one season and, as each person will typically eat ten to fifteen crayfish in one sitting and the local variety is so expensive, hosting a party serving only local stock would set you back the price of a small island. Some people still fish their own, although it is a tricky affair as these creatures are nocturnal and require carefully set traps and the availability of a boat, a lake, and people who know the good spots.

To cook crayfish the Nordic way, you need to cook them live, in a brine mixed with crown dill, which is dill that has flowered, making it extra-fragrant. Most people buy the crayfish frozen, pre-cooked with dill, and just thaw and serve. This is to avoid having 150 of the critters crawling around your kitchen while you wonder if you have a pot big enough to fit them all.

Long communal tables are set with paper lanterns depicting a smiley moon, napkins and tablecloths and there are paper hats and bibs depicting crayfish for guests. The bibs are quite useful as crayfish are messy to eat. The crayfish is served cold, in big bowls in the middle of the table. Alongside these are baskets of crusty bread, crispbread, some cheese and dips for the crayfish. The sole purpose of the bread is to soak up the alcohol and ensure people don't get ideas about skinny dipping before everybody has finished eating.

A true Swede will be an expert peeler and will show off their peeling skills in the same way they manoeuvre around an IKEA showroom, making it look blissfully easy. Anyone else will struggle to twist the head off the crayfish and to get the meat out of the teeny little claws. You may find that Swedes slurp loudly, while sucking on the belly of the crayfish. The aim of this is to suck the brine from the shell, as it tastes nice. The louder the slurping, the better.

No *kräftskiva* is complete without aquavit. Bottles of the golden stuff are placed on the tables and *nubbar* are toasted. The saying goes 'one shot for every claw' but this is just a saying; if you had one for every crayfish, you'd be singing 'Dancing Queen' way too early.

A *kräftskiva* is a lovely, messy affair and a fitting ode to the humble crayfish. Being outside in nature, enjoying the last bit of light before the autumn sets in, signals the end of the Scandinavian summer and the beginning of hibernation. What better way to start than by sharing drink and food with good friends, whilst wearing bibs and silly hats?

Thank you

Being asked to write my thoughts on what it means to be a Scandinavian is a great honour – thank you Melissa Smith at Aurum Press for the idea, vision and immense support. Thank you also to Anna Jacobsen from wearehere-now for the amazing photography and Lucy Panes for the illustrations: you brought the book to life. Jane Birch for amazing editing. To my wonderful agent Jane Graham Maw and PR gals at Samphire.

Through the years of running our café ScandiKitchen we have learnt so much about what it means to be a Scandinavian, mostly from looking back in on Norway, Denmark and Sweden as ex-pats and listening to others when they question the way we do things in the north. Thank you to all the thousands of people who interact with us on social media and newsletters about our observations. Your constant comments and feedback have helped shape this book. While we know not everyone will agree with every comment, we hope you all find some smiles between the lines.

Jonas, my husband, who has the patience of a saint and lovingly picks up the pieces when this author falls apart. Astrid and Elsa, my two daughters, I hope one day that you, as Swedes born abroad, can find some fun use in this book – and a connection to strengthen your roots.

This book was written throughout a hot summer, with a lot of coffee and support of many people. David Jørgensen, my dearest friend and writing partner – thank you for being a rock and all your contributions. You never miss the details and I am forever grateful for all of the fantastic work you do and the help you give. Martina Wade, for all your help on the Norway chapters – your insight, contributions and words have all been invaluable.

My parents Lena and Niels, sisters Isa, Ginny, Lone and Ulla who took care of the kids while I fretted about word count. Annika, Andy, Joshua, Leif and Eva Aurell– you are all so supportive and have made me feel like an honorary Swede (I'm especially grateful to Leif for showing me the way on correct cheese slicing). Whilst hiding and writing in Luxembourg, thank you Dessie Quigg, Valerie Coulon, Patricia Eser, Gearóid O'Sullivan and David J. James. Back in Blighty: Helle Kaiser-Nielsen, Birgitte Agger-Mote, Hannah Ventura, Elisabeth Baldwin, David Holberton and Eva Papesch.

Last but not least: to all our lovely team at ScandiKitchen – you are the guys who make it all possible and we thank you for sharing this journey with us.

For all of their help whilst working on this project, Anna would like to thank:

Tom and Otto

My Parents, Elisabeth and Mads

Alessandro Monaco

Helena and her boys

Caroline Richter

Trine and family

Ingrid Kelfbäck

Melissa Smith

Everyone at Solgården, Borgehage

Sibbarps Kallbadhus

Bamse and family

Sara Kapusta

Creatively Independent

Brimming with creative inspiration, how-to projects and useful information to enrich your everyday life, Quarto Knows is a favourite destination for those pursuing their interests and passions. Visit our site and dig deeper with our books into your area of interest: Quarto Creates, Quarto Cooks, Quarto Homes, Quarto Lives, Quarto Drives, Quarto Explores, Quarto Gifts, or Quarto Kids.

First published in 2017 by Aurum Press, an imprint of The Quarto Group.
The Old Brewery, 6 Blundell Street, London N7 9BH, United Kingdom.
www.QuartoKnows.com

A catalogue record for this book is available from the British Library.

ISBN 978 1 78131 652 8
eISBN 978 1 78131 738 9
10 9 8 7 6 5 4 3 2 1
2021 2020 2019 2018 2017
Printed in China